What Have the Irish Ever Done for Us?

David Forsythe

Illustrated by Alba Esteban

First published in 2019 by Currach Press
23 Merrion Square
Dublin 2
Ireland
www.currachbooks.com

ISBN: 978-1-78218-904-6

Set in Gill Sans 9/13 and KG Two Is Better Than One
Illustrations and Book design by Alba Esteban | Currach Press
All other images © Wikimedia Commons
Printed by Jellyfish Solutions

CURRACH
PRESS

WHAT HAVE THE IRISH EVER DONE FOR US?

DAVID FORSYTHE

ILLUSTRATED BY ALBA ESTEBAN

CURRACH PRESS

TO MY WIFE, MARY

ABOUT THE AUTHOR

Scriptwriter, author and journalist David Forsythe has had a varied career as a reporter, feature writer, scriptwriter, newspaper and online editor.

He has worked as a local reporter in Cork city and was editor of the *Cork Independent* newspaper before founding a successful news agency providing copy for national and international media.

He founded the *West Cork Times* online newspaper in West Cork and more recently has developed a career as a scriptwriter for film and television, writing a prime time documentary series for RTÉ. He is a director of the film production company Wet Rocks Media where he is responsible for script development.

In 2017 he was the author of *The Celtic Songlines*, the book accompanying the RTÉ television series which he also wrote, presented by Dónal Lunny.

The son of an Irish mother and English father, he was born and brought up in London and throughout his career has been fascinated by the influences that shape our cultural identity.

He lives in West Cork, Ireland with his wife and five children.

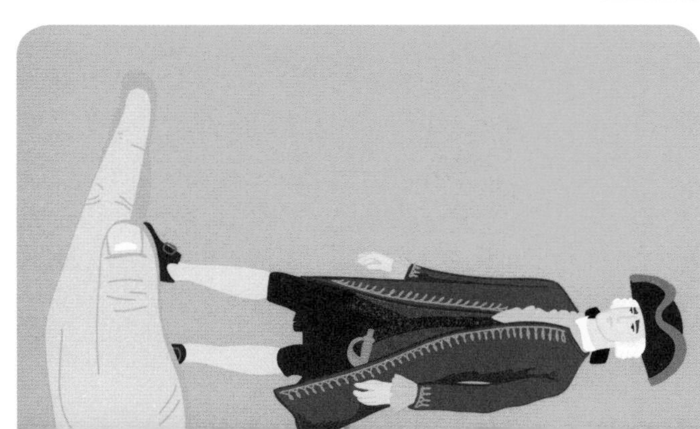

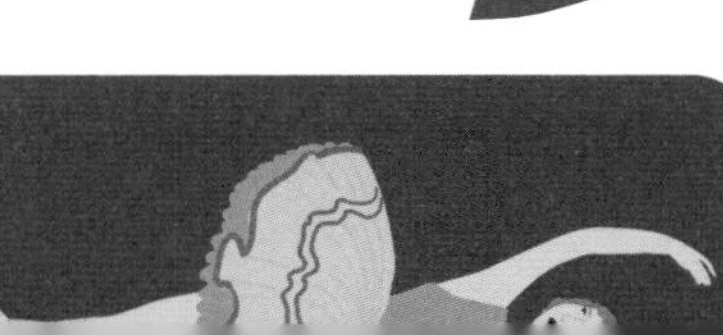

CONTENTS

INTRODUCTION

The idea for this book came about in 2013 during a tourism initiative developed by the Irish Government known as 'The Gathering Ireland'. The plan was to mark 2013 with a number of events, big and small, across the country to welcome home the children of Ireland's far-flung diaspora.

As a reporter working in Ireland I was ambivalent at best about the initiative, but in the course of my work I was obliged to attend several of the planned 'gatherings'. The idea grew on me as I learned more about some of the fascinating and famous people who have come out of Ireland's towns, villages and townlands. Some of the stories were fanciful, but many were fascinating tales that I had never heard before. I collected quite a few of these stories in the course of the year, many of which have made it into this book.

But as I was writing this book I realised that simply listing a number of Irish people who have done well for themselves isn't interesting unless those people have made a real difference to the lives of others. The famous scene in Monty Python's *Life of Brian* sprang to mind, when John Cleese's character Reg asks his disgruntled Judean freedom fighters what the Romans have ever done for them – as it turned out, quite a lot! It also turns out that the Irish have done quite a lot for us too, and researching the achievements of Irish people made me realise just how much the Irish have achieved.

During the course of my research, another question also kept popping into my head: when we say Irish, whom do we actually mean? Defining Irishness is a notoriously difficult (and contentious) thing to do. In the post-1916 isolationist Ireland, it has often meant Irish and Catholic. What struck me, however, was just how much Anglicans, Presbyterians, Baptists, Methodists, Quakers and others to the North and South had also achieved. It is these people, along with the Anglo-Irish gentry, the old Norman nobility, the Catholic tenant farmers, northern Unionists and all the other people that have hailed from Ireland, that make the country what it is. The Irish are those who were born here, made here or who feel they belong here – they have all played their part and were all shaped by this unique place. This book highlights just how important their contributions have been not just to Ireland, but also to the world as a whole.

ENGINEERING PIONEERS

At the end of the 19th Century and into the early 20th Century, major advances were being made in the fields of steam power, mechanics and electrical engineering. These developments improved upon earlier, more primitive technologies and helped make the Industrial Revolution possible. Among the many engineers and inventors who played their part in this exciting age of innovation were several Irishmen.

JAMES J. WOOD

Bridge pioneer

Born in Kinsale, County Cork in 1856, James J. Wood immigrated to the United States with his family when he was eight-years-old. The family settled in Connecticut, and from an early age Wood showed a remarkable talent for engineering. At just 11-years-old he began working for a lock-making company in Branford, Connecticut!. He then moved to New York in 1864 and took a job with the Brady engineering company in Brooklyn, where he was quickly recognised for his skills.

Wood worked on three of the most innovative inventions in the 19th Century: suspension bridges, elevators and refrigerators. He designed the machine that made the cables for the Brooklyn Bridge, the world's first steel wire suspension bridge; this technology would later be used to make cables for elevators in the new skyscrapers of the day. His electrical company was bought by the Fort Wayne Electric Corporation in 1890 and was later absorbed into General Electric, today one of the world's largest and most profitable firms. In later years he also played a key role in the development of the domestic refrigerator that would go on to become a very successful product for General Electric.

CHARLES ALGERNON PARSONS

Mastermind of the steam turbine

Charles Algernon Parsons revolutionised modern electricity. He was born in London in 1854, the youngest of the six sons of Anglo-Irish astronomer William Parsons, the Earl of Rosse. Parsons grew up at the family estate, Birr Castle, in County Offaly. In 1866, when Parsons was just 12-years-old he is reputed to have built a steam carriage with his brothers that could travel around the castle grounds at a speedy 10 mph! He was educated at home in Offaly before reading mathematics at Trinity College in Dublin and later attending Cambridge. Following his studies, he travelled to Newcastle to work as an apprentice engineer and in 1884 he secured a job with the Clarke Chapman Company in nearby Gateshead, a major manufacturer of cranes, shipping equipment and marine engines. He became a partner at the firm and, while there, developed a major advance in steam engine technology: the steam turbine.

Steam engines of the day were inefficient and could not be used to directly generate electricity. They were also noisy, highly polluting and expensive. Parsons' multi-stage steam turbine design used a system that generates power from a circular turbine that transformed the production of electricity, as well as marine engine design. His design proved to be vastly superior to existing technologies and was able to generate electricity at a much lower cost than previous versions. His invention was such a breakthrough that he left his job to set up his own company, C.A. Parsons & County, in Newcastle to concentrate on producing steam turbines. Parsons developed and refined his designs and began producing turbines for use in power stations.

Parsons was also convinced that turbines could be used on ships to provide far more efficient power generation. In 1897 he launched his own vessel, the 100-foot 'Turbinia' that was fitted with a steam turbine of his design. The Parsons steam turbine was soon in use in numerous naval vessels and ocean liners, including the RMS Lusitania and HMS Dreadnought. Thanks to Parsons, steam turbines became the dominant form of propulsion for decades. Parsons was made a fellow of the Royal Society in 1898 and was knighted in 1911 for his contribution to engineering. He died in 1931 while on a cruise in the West Indies. The company he founded went on to become one of the biggest employers in the industrial heartland of Tyneside and eventually merged with the Clarke Chapman Company before becoming part of Rolls Royce, and today is part of the Siemens group. His achievements are remembered at a museum at his family home in Birr Castle, County Offaly.

HARRY FERGUSON

Agricultural revolutionary

Modern farming would not exist without a particularly industrious Irishman by the name of Harry Ferguson. Born in 1884, Ferguson was a farm boy from a large Protestant family who grew up in the beautiful rolling countryside near Dromore in County Down, and he developed a keen interest in engineering at a young age.

Known as something of a dreamer in his younger days, Ferguson almost immigrated to Canada as a young man but was offered a job by his brother, who had set up his own successful mechanic's business in Belfast. Ferguson decided against emigration and in 1902 he headed to Belfast to begin work with his brother Joe. He worked on everything from bicycles to the new-fangled motorcars.

Ferguson is most famous for developing and engineering his own plough attachment that could be mounted directly on the back of the common Ford Eros tractor of the time. Known as the Belfast Plough, it was the first wheel-less plough to enter production. This technical advance made tractors far more efficient, and the system quickly became an industry standard and is still used on the vast majority of tractors to this day.

Not content to just manufacture tractor attachments, Ferguson also developed his own prototype – the Ferguson 'Black' tractor - to demonstrate the device, and the tractor went into production in 1936 as the Ferguson 'Model A'. In 1938 Ferguson travelled to Michigan and met with Henry Ford, hoping to branch out into the American market. Ford, himself the son of an Irish Protestant immigrant from County Cork, was impressed by Ferguson's design and the two struck a 'handshake agreement' that led to the production of the Ford-Ferguson 9N in 1939. Today Ferguson's memory lives on, as in many parts of the world a tractor is often known as a 'Fergie'.

HENRY FORD

Vehicular miracle-worker

Ford Model 'T' car no. 2, winner of the trans-continental race from New York to Seattle, arriving at the Alaska Yukon Pacific Exposition, Seattle, June 1909.

Though many of us take our cars for granted, modern vehicles would not exist without the manufacturing genius that was Henry Ford. Though Henry himself was born in Greenfield, Michigan in 1863, his father William was born in the village of Ballinascarthy, near the town of Clonakilty outside of Cork. As a child, Henry loved taking apart the pocket watch his father gave him to see how all the parts fitted together, and gained a reputation as a watch repairman among his neighbours and friends. In 1879, he moved to Detroit to apprentice as a machinist, eventually going on to work a variety of industrial jobs. He became chief engineer at the Edison Illuminating Company, but in his spare time he indulged his passion for developing a gasoline engine and, after much trial and error, in 1896 he came up with the self-propelled Ford Quadricycle. Ford was also involved in the development of racing cars, and in 1902 he designed the Ford 999, which broke the land speed record. He teamed up with coal baron Alexander Malcomson, who gave him the financial backing to produce this new, cheap car, and The Ford Motor Company was officially formed in 1903. When the company was formed, the Ford 999 was brought on a tour of the country, providing excellent advertising for the new brand.

But it was Ford's next design, the Model T, and the manner in which he built it, that proved truly revolutionary. The Model T was launched in 1908 as a cheap, modern family car, easy to drive and inexpensive to fix. In 1913 Ford created a revolutionary production system to produce the car: the assembly line, which drove down production costs while increasing efficiency and speed. The Model T was a huge success and became ubiquitous on America's streets. Ford sold 15,000,000 Model Ts in total, becoming a multibillionaire and founding one of America's industrial giants in the process.

The company expanded internationally, but Ford never forgot his ancestral homeland. He opened a major tractor factory in Cork in 1917 that was a mainstay of the Irish economy for decades. It was Ford's first purpose-built factory outside America, and at one stage in the 1920s it was reputedly the largest tractor plant in the world.

Ford

JOHN BOYD DUNLOP
WILLIAM HARVEY DU CROS

JOHN BOYD DUNLOP & WILLIAM HARVEY DU CROS

The pneumatic men

The advent of the mass-produced motorcar in the early 20th Century transformed the world and the way people moved, but without a simple innovation developed in Ireland, this transportation revolution could not have happened. Before there were motorcars powered by the internal combustion engine, there were a variety of steam and electrically powered vehicles, but none was a serious alternative to horse powered vehicles as a practical form of transport for the masses. Even the early motorcars had a serious shortcoming: the quality of the ride. Most vehicles used wooden or metal wheels and suffered from the same problem: they produced a harsh and bumpy ride that not only shook the passengers, but also the vehicles themselves, causing damage and wear at an alarming rate.

It was a Belfast veterinarian by the name of John Boyd Dunlop who unwittingly came up with the innovation that would make the age of the motorcar possible. Dunlop was a Scot who had moved to Downpatrick in County Down to set up a veterinary practice in 1867. In 1888 he developed a pneumatic/air-filled tyre for use on his son's tricycle. His ten-year-old son had been getting headaches from riding his trike on the rough pavements of 19th Century Belfast, and with the help of the child's doctor, John Fagan, Dunlop set about designing a tyre that would give the tricycle a smoother and more comfortable ride. The little trike's performance and ride were greatly enhanced by the new tyres, so Dunlop decided to patent the idea.

His innovation was timely, because at around the same time the safety bicycle, or what we would know of as the modern bicycle, was also introduced. Prior to that, penny-farthings with a giant front wheel were the common bicycles of the day. They were dangerous to ride and gave cyclists a bone-shaking cycling experience! The safety bicycle was a huge hit and caused bike sales to rise dramatically. Racing cyclists also began to take an interest in the Dunlop tyre, believing it could give them an advantage in competition.

It was at this point that William Harvey du Cros, the man who was ultimately responsible for making Dunlop's idea an international success, entered the story. He managed the cycling team, 'The Invincibles', which his sons were a part of, and he was also the president of the Irish Cycling Association. In 1889 the captain of the Belfast Cruisers Cycling Club, Willie Hume, began using Dunlop's tyres on his racing bike and in May of that same year he won all four events at the Queen's College Sports in Belfast. Two of du Cros's sons were among those in the field beaten by Dunlop's pneumatic tyres, and du Cros was immediately fascinated by Dunlop's innovation.

He approached Dunlop to explore the possibility of producing pneumatic tyres on a mass scale. Dunlop agreed and they further developed the product for the mass market, re-establishing the Booth Brothers Company as the Pneumatic Tyre and Booth's Cycle Agency in the process, though the company name would later change to Dunlop Rubber. The Dunlop Rubber Company manufactured its first car tyre in 1900. William Harvey du Cros employed his six sons to promote the business at various locations around the world and several factories were opened in the following years, including a major facility in Cork in the south of Ireland.

ALEXANDER MITCHELL

Lighthouse architect

For ships seeking safe harbour around the world, sandbanks and mudflats have always been a problem. They are hard to spot and have been responsible for numerous vessels running aground and sinking. It is also difficult to warn vessels of these problem areas, because mudflats and sandbanks aren't suitable places for lighthouses that could alert ships of trouble ahead. It was an Irish engineer by the name of Alexander Mitchell who came up with a simple and economical solution to this problem.

Mitchell was born in Dublin in 1780, the son of the Inspector-General of Army Barracks in Ireland. When he was seven-years-old, he moved with his parents and siblings to Pine Hill, near Belfast. The city was Alexander's home for the rest of his life. His eyesight had always been poor and by the time he was sixteen he was no longer able to read, and by the age of twenty-two he was blind. Despite his disability, Mitchell was an outgoing and optimistic man. His blindness did not hold him back from providing for his family, and he established a successful brick-making business in the Ballymacarrett area of Belfast. It was while running his business that he developed a flair for engineering, and he established a number of innovations to aid in the brick-making process.

Back then, Belfast was a major port and a shipbuilding city, so Mitchell was no doubt well acquainted with the problems of sandbanks, and he came up with an ingenious and simple innovation that had a major impact on harbours around the world. In 1833 Mitchell patented a new design that made it possible to erect a lighthouse virtually anywhere. He designed the screw-pile lighthouse, which was inspired by a simple wine corkscrew. The design consisted of a 20-foot-long iron pile with a four-foot wide screw helix at the bottom end.

His screw-pile design made constructing lighthouses and warning beacons on sandbanks both practical and relatively cheap. The lighthouse design was typically octagonal with one central pile and eight others arranged around it to support the structure above. In 1838 Mitchell was contracted to erect a screw-pile lighthouse at Maplin Sands in the Thames Estuary near London, the first of many over the following years. Despite his blindness, Mitchell acted as consultant for the installation of most of his lighthouses and was said to enjoy singing along with the workers and showed no fear of falling into the water, which he did on at least two occasions!

Several screw-pile lighthouses were erected around the Irish and British coasts including at Cork Harbour, Wexford, Dundalk, Morecambe Bay, Sheerness, Fleetwood and Belfast. However, it was abroad that his screw-pile design proved to be an even greater success. In the USA, the new breakwater in Portland, Oregon was constructed using screw piles; screw-pile lighthouses also dotted along the whole of the East Coast of the USA. In India and Japan, the design also proved highly popular, and was used for a wide range of structures including railway bridges, telegraph poles and viaducts. Screw-piles also became the common attachment type for securing boat moorings. Today screw-piles are widely used for a variety of building applications, and many of those original screw-pile lighthouses still survive, including the Spit Bank Lighthouse in Cork Harbour.

MILITARY ENGINEERS

The Irish contribution to military engineering has been significant, with the tank and submarine both invented by Irishmen. Indeed, modern warfare would not be what it is today without these inventions. Here we look at the creation stories of these two inventions and their inventors.

JOHN HOLLAND

Inventor of the submarine

As unlikely as it may seem, the modern submarine is indeed an Irish invention, developed by the talented John P. Holland from Liscannor in County Clare. Born in 1841, Holland was the son of the local coastguard, and spent his formative years living in the coastguard's cottage overlooking the Atlantic Ocean. The sea was obviously a constant in Holland's life, and some accounts also cite the influence of Jules Verne's *20,000 Leagues Under the Sea* as an inspiration for his designs. Before Holland turned his hand to inventing full-time, he was a teacher in various places in Ireland including Cork, and it was there that he drew up his first submarine designs in 1859 that formed the basis of his successful prototype almost 20 years later.

He immigrated to the United States in 1873 and after a short spell with an engineering firm, he returned to teaching at St John's School in Paterson, New Jersey. He eventually gave up teaching to concentrate on submarine design full-time and launched his first real-life submarine, the 'Holland I' into New Jersey's Passiac River in 1877. A large crowd gathered to view the spectacle, but to Holland's dismay the one-man submarine began to sink as soon as it was launched! After investigations, however, it became clear that there was no problem with the design; the sub was letting in water because someone had forgotten to replace two watertight screw plugs in the hull. The next day the Holland I completed several successful dives.

In 1897 the Holland VI was launched, the vessel that would secure Holland's place in history as the father of the modern submarine. This model's major innovation was its successful use of an electric motor for underwater propulsion and a petrol engine for use when surfaced; the vessel also included a reloadable torpedo tube and was the first truly capable submarine of the kind we would recognise today.

The US Navy purchased the Holland VI in 1900 where the vessel became the USS Holland, the first commissioned submarine, and ordered six more to form the world's first naval submarine fleet. This success led other navies to purchase the design, including Japan, and the United Kingdom. The Holland Torpedo Boat Company became the Electric Boat Company, which then became General Dynamics, now one of the world's biggest defence contractors, but Holland left the company he founded in 1904. He died in New Jersey in 1914 at the beginning of the First World War, where his invention revolutionised naval warfare forever.

WALTER WILSON

Originator of the tank

Born in Blackrock, County Dublin in 1874, Walter Gordon Wilson is credited with designing the first modern tank to enter active service. He was a talented engineer and became a naval cadet before studying mechanical science at Cambridge University, graduating with a first-class degree in 1897. When the First World War broke out in 1914 he re-joined the navy and was assigned to the Royal Naval Armoured Car Division due to his engineering expertise. As the brutal reality of trench warfare became apparent, commanders on both sides were desperate to find a technological solution that could break the bloody stalemate. In 1915, the First Lord of the Admiralty, Winston Churchill established The Landships Committee, which was tasked with developing an armoured fighting vehicle for use on the Western Front.

Wilson, with his proven engineering knowledge, was assigned to the task, along with Englishman William Tritton, an agricultural engineer who had experience designing tractors. Wilson and Tritton came up with the first modern tank design, an armed and armoured prototype called 'Little Willie' that used caterpillar tracks for traction to prevent the vehicle from sinking into the mud. Wilson suggested extending the tracks around the entire machine, and it was this design that formed the basis of the Mark I tank. The first Mark I tanks went into action at the Battle of the Somme in September 1916; it was the first time a tank had been used in warfare. Wilson and Tritton made several improvements and advances to the design of the tank, and many variants saw action before the end of the war in 1918.

An early model British Mark I 'male' tank, named C-15, near Thiepval, 25 September 1916. The tank is probably in reserve for the Battle of Thiepval Ridge which began on 26 September. The tank is fitted with the wire 'grenade shield' and steering tail, both features discarded in the next models.

IRELAND IN FLIGHT

These days air travel is often viewed as more of a chore than a pleasure by most people, so it is hard to imagine the excitement felt around the world following the first powered flight by the American Wright brothers in 1903. These 'magnificent men with their flying machines' gripped the world's attention, and many Irish men and women turned their fascination into bonafide careers.

JAMES MARTIN

Architect of the ejector seat

Born in Crossgar, County Down in 1893, James Martin's contribution to aviation has saved thousands of lives across the world. Martin, later Sir James Martin, grew up on a farm in the Ulster countryside. Though his father died when he was a young boy, his older brother encouraged his inventive streak, and Martin was already an accomplished, self-taught engineer in his teenage years. After attending an interview at Queens University in Belfast, the professor and Martin apparently agreed that he would be better off out in the world of work, making things, rather than studying in a stuffy lecture hall!

Soon afterwards Martin moved to London, aiming to set up his own engineering business. With no contacts and little money, he found a suitable shed in the Acton area of West London, bought some tools and materials and set to work. It was a one-man show, and Martin had to do everything from design to deliveries. Despite these obstacles, he managed to make a success of his fledgling business and became well known for developing custom engines and vehicles. Martin also developed an interest in flight, and soon turned his attention to aircraft safety. In 1944 he was asked by the Ministry of Defence to look into possible solutions to help pilots escape from aircrafts when in trouble. Martin came up with the basis for the modern ejector seat, concluding that the only way to save somebody from a crashing aircraft was to fire them clear out of the vehicle, but still in their seat, using explosives.

Several prototypes were designed and tested, first from a static position on the ground and later from a moving aircraft. The first static test took place on January 24th 1945 when Bernard Lynch successfully ejected. Lynch was also the first to use an ejector seat in flight on July 24th 1946. With many subsequent successful tests completed, the Martin-Baker ejector seat went into production and was used for the first time in an emergency on May 30th 1949, when Jo Lancaster ejected from an Armstrong Whitworth AW52 over Warwickshire.

The Martin-Baker Aircraft Company is to this day a leading manufacturer of ejection seats, with operations in England, France, Italy and the United States. They supply ejection seats for more than 90 air forces and their seats are fitted to more than 200 types of aircraft. Martin-Baker says that since the first successful use of the seat in 1949, 7,450 lives have been saved by the company's ejection seats. James died in 1981 and is commemorated with a memorial in the town square in Crossgar and was also featured on the Northern Bank £100 note in Northern Ireland. The Martin-Baker Company continues to be run by his two sons.

BRENDAN O'REGAN

Duty-free designer

Born just a few miles from the airport in Sixmilebridge, County Clare in 1917, Brendan O'Regan was a true visionary who revolutionised airports as we know them today. His background was in hospitality, having worked as the head of catering at the Foynes seaplane base. When the new Shannon Airport in the area opened, he was the obvious choice to take on the same role, and was appointed in 1945. But O'Regan did so much more than just run the catering at the airport. He came up with the idea of duty-free airport sales.

O'Regan saw that the numbers of passengers passing through the airport were growing rapidly, but there was little reason for them to spend any time or money in the airport. His idea to exploit this market of potential customers was simple: allow the airport to sell valuable gift items and goods to these passengers at reduced tax rates. The government agreed to give the idea a try, and in 1947 the Customs Free Airport Act was passed in the Irish parliament, establishing Shannon as the world's first duty-free airport. It was an immediate hit with passengers and was quickly copied at airports around the world.

O'Regan continued to play a major role at home becoming the head of the Irish Tourism Board and also a peace campaigner for improving relations between the Republic and Northern Ireland.

LILIAN BLAND

Female flight pioneer

Born in Maidstone, Kent, England in 1878, Lilian Bland came from a respected Anglo-Irish family and became the first woman in Ireland, and one of the first women in the world, to design, build and fly her own airplane. Bland's early career was as a photographer and journalist in London, and she was well known for her non-conformist attitude, refusing to behave as young ladies of the day were expected to.

She moved to her aunt Sarah's home of Tobercorran House, Carnmoney near Belfast with her father at the turn of the century. Her interest in aviation began when her uncle Robert sent her a postcard from Paris that featured the new Blériot monoplane. At the time, the only way she could possibly take to the air herself was to build her own aircraft, so that's exactly what she set about doing.

Lilian began researching the early flight pioneers and their aircrafts, gathering as much information as she could, and first built a scale model of the machine she proposed to fly. She then developed the idea into a flyable, full-size glider that was ready for testing in 1910. She named the new biplane the 'Mayfly' and began testing it on Carnmoney Hill, adapting and developing the design and eventually adding a petrol engine.

Testing moved to Randalstown, near Antrim, and it was here that Bland made her first successful flight in August 1910; it was a short distance, but it was also a confirmed, powered flight. The achievement made her the first woman to fly an airplane in Ireland, and hers was also the first powered flight by a biplane in Ireland. She continued to refine her aircraft and considered adding a more powerful engine to the design, but ultimately was persuaded by her father to retire from aviation following her achievement.

Side view of Bland Mayfly, 1910.

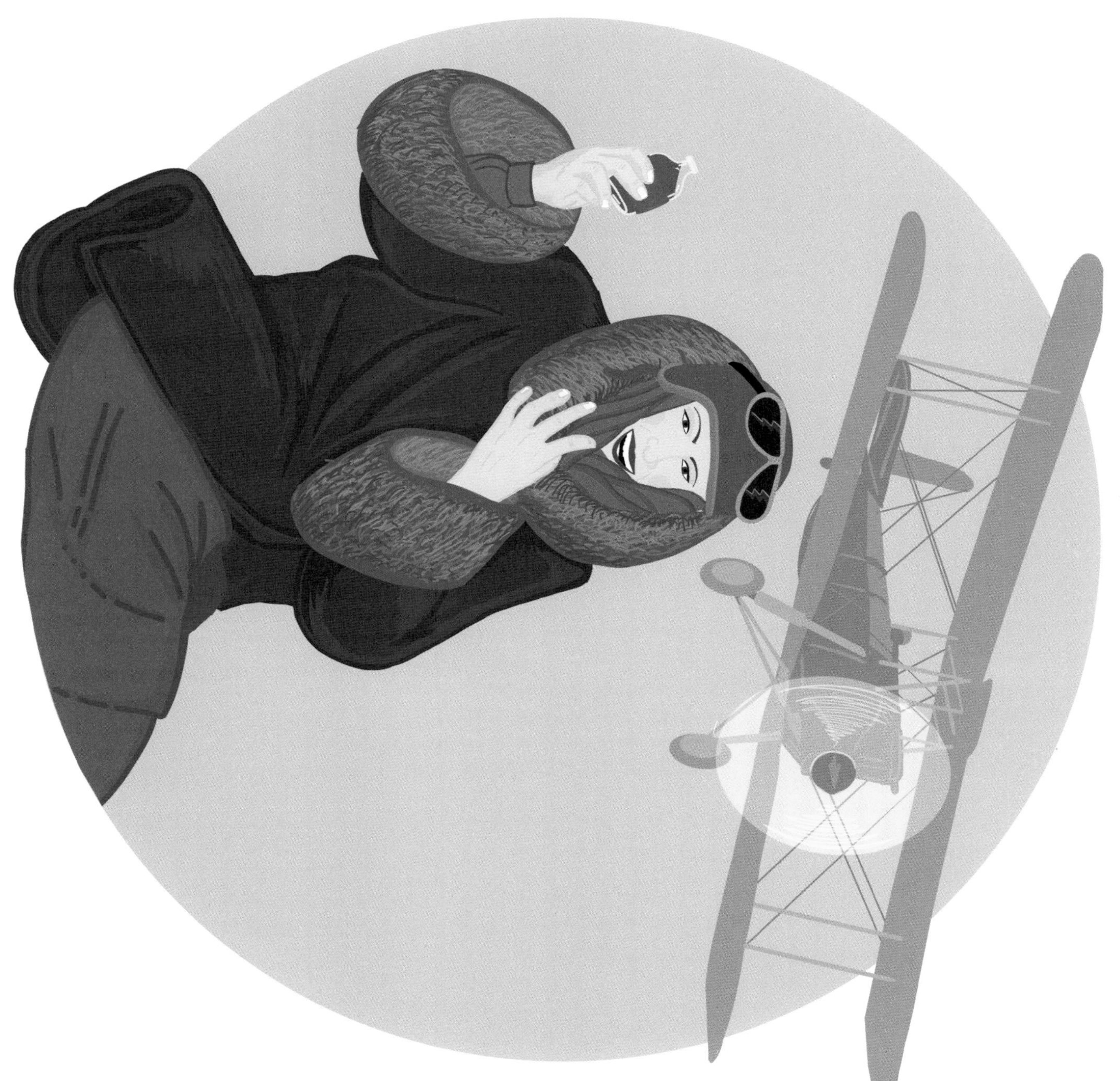

LADY MARY HEATH

Transcontinental pilot

The story of Limerick aviator Lady Mary Heath is one of short-lived superstardom. During the age of the aviation pioneers, hers was a name that was mentioned alongside Amelia Earhart or Charles Lindbergh. She was the first person to fly solo from Cape Town, South Africa to London.

She was born Sophie Peirce-Evans at Knockaderry House near Newcastle West, County Limerick in 1896. She studied at the Royal College of Science in Dublin. Sophie was a talented athlete, and while at the Royal College she was a founder of the Women's Amateur Athletic Association. She became Britain's first women's javelin champion and was a delegate to the 1925 International Olympic Committee. She also represented Britain at the Women's Olympiad in Monte Carlo and the 1926 Women's World Games in Gothenburg, taking part in a number of events. It was around this time that she began to take flying lessons and discovered her true passion in life: aviation.

Sophie's first long-distance flight was in 1925, when she flew to Prague to attend the eighth Olympic Congress. It was the last congress attended by Olympics founder Pierre de Coubertin as president, and Sophie petitioned him and fellow Olympic Council members to admit women to compete in the events; as a result, women were allowed to compete for the first time at the 1928 games in Amsterdam. In 1927 she married Sir James Heath, becoming Lady Mary Heath in the process.

She soon became the first woman in Britain to hold a commercial flying licence and began to set a number of flying records, but no airline would employ her because of societal prejudice against women at the time. She was also the first woman to complete a parachute jump from an aircraft and to complete a loop-the-loop! In 1928 she made her crowning achievement: she became the first pilot (male or female) to complete the gruelling flight from Cape Town, South Africa to London. The journey took her three months and was completed in the Avro Avian aircraft her new husband had bought for her. She encountered numerous problems along the way, including heatstroke and being shot at in Libya.

On her return she was greeted as a heroine and thousands turned out to see her at Croydon Aerodrome, which was then London's main airport. Mary instantly became one of the most recognisable people in the world, a genuine star of aviation's golden age. But Amelia Earhart, who became the first woman to fly across the Atlantic, soon eclipsed her fame. Not content to fade from the limelight completely, Mary eventually set up her own aviation business near Dublin and was responsible for training many of the first employees of the new Irish state airline, Aer Lingus.

WORKPLACE INVENTIONS

Necessity is often the mother of invention, and this was certainly the case with some of the inventions created by Ireland's brightest countrymen. They identified a need for equipment in the workplace, set about inventing it, and in the process, made history. Here are a few of their stories.

WILLIAM REID CLANNY

Mining safety promoter

A miner tests for flammable gas using a safety lamp.

A physician by profession, William Reid Clanny from Bangor in County Down made a major contribution to the safety of coalminers across the world. Born in 1776, Clanny trained as a physician in Edinburgh and joined the Royal Navy. He eventually settled in Durham, England. At the time the area around Newcastle had become one of the world's major coal producing regions, and Clanny moved the short distance north to the growing industrial town of Sunderland where he was to live and work for the rest of his life. Coal mining was one of the major industries of the area; it was tough and dangerous work and men were regularly killed in pit explosions caused by methane gas being ignited by the candles and lamps used by the miners. The problem of providing safe lighting in the mines was a difficult one that many had tried and failed to solve over the years—they even tried using bioluminescent fish skins and bottled fireflies to see in the mines!

Gaining inspiration from the mining community around him, Clanny set about designing a 'safety lamp' that would use still use candlelight but would isolate the flame from the surrounding atmosphere, thus preventing fatal explosions. His initial design placed the candle within a glass case sat on top of a water container through which air was forced using a bellows to provide oxygen, and a separate chamber above to allow fumes escape as bubbles. The early designs were cumbersome, but they did work, and he refined them substantially to make them more portable.

His innovations were also noted by others working to solve the same problem, and within a few years miners across the world were using safety lamps that greatly improved safety and reduced the number of explosions. Clanny stayed in Sunderland and continued to take an interest in helping to improve working conditions and safety for miners.

THOMAS NESBITT

Inventor of the harpoon gun

Whales of several types are frequent visitors to the Irish coasts, and today there is a thriving tourism industry based around whale watching. In the 18th and 19th centuries, however, whales were not watched, but utilised, and the whaling industry produced such prized commodities as whale blubber, oil, meat and bones. One of the first commercial whaling operations in Ireland was at Inver on Donegal Bay. The whale fishery there was established by Thomas Nesbitt, a member of the well-known Nesbitt family of Woodstown House who emigrated to Donegal from Scotland in the 17th Century.

Whaling did not truly develop into a large-scale commercial operation until the mid 18th Century. Nesbitt, who was born in 1729, had noted the numerous whales often sighted off the coast of his native Donegal and decided to establish a fishery himself with the help of his brother and a number of local men. The Donegal whaling station was set up in 1759 when Thomas purchased a 140-ton whaling vessel in London. After having five whaling boats made, he hired a number of experienced whalers and set up shore facilities at the port of Inver, near Killybegs. Following a poor initial season, Thomas successfully petitioned parliament in London for financial aid to improve his station's facilities. It is at around this time that Arthur Young attributes the invention of the whale harpoon gun to Nesbitt in his *Tour in Ireland 1776–78* in 1780. He says of the harpoon gun, "From many experiments he brought the operation to such perfection that, for some years he never missed a whale, nor failed of holding her by the harpoon". The whale gun was further developed in the Scandinavian whaling grounds and it greatly improved the efficiency and safety of whaling. Thomas Nesbitt died in 1801 at the age of 72 and is buried in the old graveyard in Inver close to where the ruins of the old whaling station remain.

HUMPHREY O'SULLIVAN

A smart sole

Born in Skibbereen, West Cork in 1853, Humphrey O'Sullivan would go on to found one of America's most successful rubber and plastics companies, all thanks to a simple innovation that was originally intended to make his working day a bit more comfortable! After finishing school, Humphrey took a five-year apprenticeship as a printer in Cork and then founded a job in a print shop in the city. Soon after, he joined his brother in Lowell, Massachusetts, a town with a significant Irish population. O'Sullivan worked as a printer for a newspaper. It was while working at this job that O'Sullivan came up with the idea that would make his fortune. Printers spent all day on their feet standing on a stone floor tending and setting the printing presses, and it was hard on the heels. Humphrey brought a rubber mat to work with him to stand on but his colleagues kept taking it to use themselves. Fed up with chasing after his mats, Henry decided to cut two pieces of rubber from one and attach them directly to the heels of his shoes. The results impressed him so much that O'Sullivan patented the idea in 1899 and left his printing job to set about making his new rubber heels into a commercial enterprise.

Humphrey established the O'Sullivan Rubber Company and it was immediately successful, becoming one of the leading producers of rubber products, not just heels, in the USA. The company later expanded into vinyl and plastic products and to this day is a successful manufacturing company making everything from instrument panel covers for cars to linings for swimming pools.

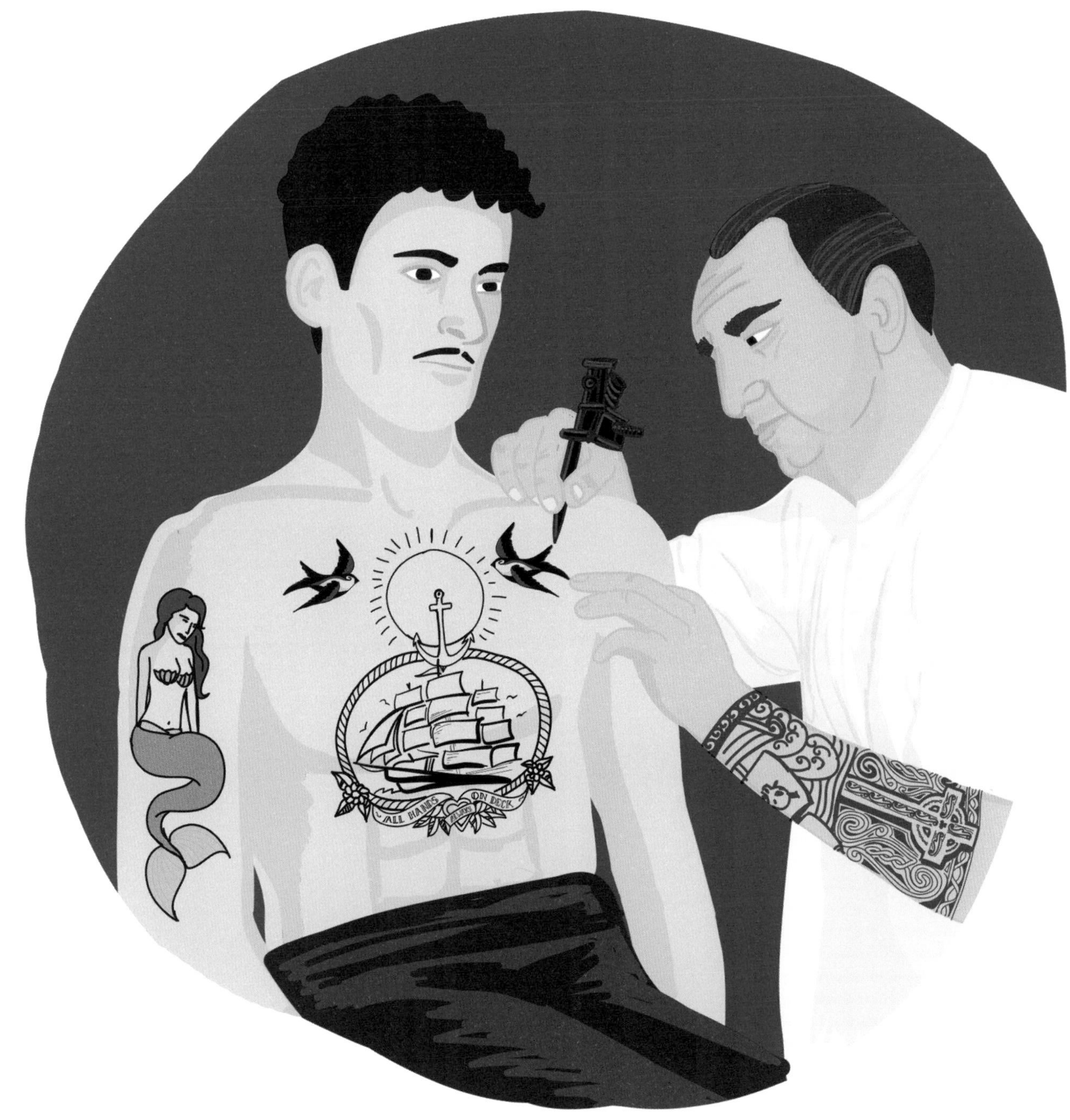
ALL HANDS
ALWAYS
ON DECK

SAMUEL O'REILLY

Tattoo trade game-changer

Once the preserve of Maori warriors and merchant seamen, it seems that nowadays every other person has a tattoo. There is evidence of tattooing going back to the earliest periods of recorded history and the practice has been widespread in many cultures around the world. It was not until the turn of the 19th Century, however, that tattooing became more common in western societies. Popular among sailors, tattoos were also worn by members of the upper classes, but were by no means common until the invention of the electric tattoo machine by an Irish American by the name of Samuel F. O'Reilly. Before O'Reilly's invention, tattooing was carried out via a set of needles usually fixed to a wooden grip used by the tattooist. The procedure was time consuming and extremely painful.

O'Reilly was one of five children born to Irish immigrant parents in Waterbury, Connecticut in 1854. In the 1880s he opened a tattoo studio in New York's Chinatown, and it is here that he had his eureka moment. The famous inventor Thomas Edison had recently demonstrated his 'autographic printing pen', a device for creating duplicate paper copies using a rotary punching mechanism. O'Reilly immediately saw the potential for this same technology to be used in tattooing and set about adapting it to create the first electric tattoo machine. Using a hollow, ink-filled needle, the machine was far more precise and delicate than the manual techniques of the time and was also much faster. He patented his design in 1891 and it proved to be an immediate success, with orders flooding in from other tattooists who wanted to get their hands on the new machine.

O'Reilly became one of the most sought-after tattooists in America. His tattooing business flourished, with patriotic Irish and American tattoos among his most popular designs. As his machine gained in popularity a number of imitators appeared on the market, and O'Reilly spent much of his time in the courts defending his patent.

IRELAND IN THE LAB

The Irish have long been keen scientists, and their studies and innovations have contributed to the development of numerous fields, including nuclear physics and seismology. Here we look at some notable examples who have advanced the field of science.

ROBERT MALLET

Father of seismology

The scientific community often refers to Robert Mallet as the 'father of seismology'. Born in Dublin, in 1810 he attended Trinity College before going on to work for his father's iron foundry as an engineer. This foundry was one of the most important in Ireland and was contracted to carry out some of the biggest civil engineering jobs of the day, such as the isolated Fastnet Lighthouse off of the coast of west Cork, also known as 'Ireland's teardrop', since it was the last Irish land many emigrants saw when sailing from Queenstown to America.

He became a member of the Royal Academy in 1832 when he was just 22-years-old and was already carrying out his own seismological research. It was in 1846 that he presented a paper entitled 'On the Dynamics of Earthquakes' that is regarded as one of the most important early scientific contributions on the subject of earthquakes. As well as making several new observations in the paper, he is also credited with coining the term 'seismology', as well as using the term 'epicentre' for the first time. He reported for the Royal Society on the devastating Basilicata earthquake of 1857 in which 11,000 people died and produced a major scientific paper on the event, using photographs of what happened in Italy to demonstrate his own theories of seismology. His pictures are believed to be the very first photographs of the aftermath of an earthquake. Mallet moved to London in 1861 where he worked as a consulting engineer and was awarded a number of industry prizes, including the Cunningham Medal of the Royal Irish Academy and the Geological Society of London's highest award, for his research into earthquakes.

Image from *Great Neapolitan Earthquake of 1857, vol.1* by Robert Mallet.

QUAKE!

FRANCIS BEAUFORT

Created his own scale

Born in Navan, County Meath, Francis Beaufort is best known today for the Beaufort Scale system of wind measurement. He left school at an early age in order to sail with the merchant navy, later transferring to the Royal Navy. He was present at the Glorious First of June, a major naval engagement between France and Britain in the southwest Ireland in 1794.

In 1805, he became commander of the HMS Woolwich and he devised the famous Beaufort Scale for categorising winds at sea. The scale ranged from 0 for calm to 13 for storm, and provided an accurate and comparable measurement. Prior to this invention, there was no universal scale for comparison, making it very difficult for ships to compare readings. Beaufort's scale overcame this problem and was standard for all vessels by the 1850s.

While commanding the Woolwich, he also began making extensive charts and was later sent to South America to carry out a hydrographic survey of the Rio de la Plata estuary. The quality of his survey work was exceptional, and he continued to the southern coast of Turkey where he charted many ancient Greek ruins accurately for the first time. By 1829 he was elected as Fellow of the Royal Astronomical Society and was appointed Chief Hydrographer for the Royal Navy, a position he held for the following 25 years, during which time he produced some of the finest charts in the world. He also developed the first reliable tide tables for the British coast, an innovation that was soon copied in other parts of the world.

In 1831 he trained Robert Fitzroy, the captain of the survey ship HMS Beagle, in his wind measurement scale. Fitzroy mentioned he was looking for a 'scientific gentleman' to join the ship for its next survey mission. Beaufort suggested a researcher he knew by the name of Charles Darwin and it was on the second voyage of the Beagle that Darwin would do much of his research on which he based his book *The Origin of Species* and the theory of evolution.

ROBERT BOYLE

Made his own laws

"The absolute pressure exerted by a given mass of an ideal gas is inversely proportional to the volume it occupies if the temperature and amount of gas remain unchanged within a closed system." Got that? This is Boyle's Law, which basically means the pressure of a gas goes up, as the container it is in gets smaller. Sounds simple, but at the time it was developed by Robert Boyle from Lismore, County Waterford it was ground breaking.

Boyle was from a wealthy land-owning family who lived at the beautiful Lismore Castle by the banks of the Blackwater River. He came from enormous wealth and privilege, but he was far from idle; in fact, Boyle was one of the most brilliant minds of his day and is regarded now as a true scientific pioneer and trailblazer. He is one of the founders of modern chemistry as well as one of the first scientists to use a modern, rigorous scientific method. After moving to Oxford in 1654 he began a series of experiments looking at the properties of gases that eventually resulted in his namesake law.

He also made discoveries relating to how sound travels through air, the qualities of freezing water and a variety of other investigations, as well as publishing what is regarded as the definitive early chemistry text, *The Sceptical Chymist* in 1661.

He was very close to his sister, who is widely acknowledged as an uncredited assistant to many of his studies, and he eventually left Oxford to live with her in London. He died in 1691, just a week after his sister predeceased him.

The Boyle Medal for Scientific Excellence awarded by the Royal Dublin Society and the *Irish Times*, is Ireland's most prestigious scientific honour and is named after Robert Boyle, and the Waterford Institute of Technology hosts an annual summer school in his honour.

WILLIAM THOMSON

Dynamic inventor of thermodynamic measurement

William Thomson, probably better known by his honorific title of Baron Kelvin of Largs, was a Belfast-born scientist and mathematician who developed the Kelvin temperature scale. He went to the University of Glasgow at the age of 10 to study; though this might seem outlandish, at that time universities and colleges in Scotland were often in competition to attract the best students, no matter their age. Following Glasgow he went on to Cambridge University where he excelled in maths and physics, but later returned to Glasgow to take on the role of Professor of Natural Philosophy.

As well as being a gifted scientist, Thomson was also an innovative and attentive teacher, introducing a number of changes to teaching practices in Glasgow, including making laboratory work part of degree courses for the first time. Always interested in practical devices, he also had a successful career as an engineer for transatlantic telegraph cables that were then connecting America and Europe for the first time. It was for his work on the first transatlantic cable that he was made Lord Kelvin.

His greatest achievement, however, was his work in thermodynamics; he played a key role in developing the Second Law of Thermodynamics. At a meeting of scientists in Oxford he came across a debate between colleagues about the convertibility of temperature readings between different substances. It set him to thinking about how to develop such a scale, and as a result, his solution was the Kelvin scale, an absolute, thermodynamic temperature scale that soon became the accepted method for measuring temperatures in science.

Sir William Thomson, Baron Kelvin, 1824 - 1907. Scientist, resting on a binnacle and holding a marine azimuth mirror. Picture from National Galleries of Scotland Commons from Edinburgh, Scotland, UK.

ALICIA BOOLE STOTT

Fourth dimension explorer

Being the daughter of the renowned mathematician George Boole and his wife, teacher Mary Everest Boole, obviously rubbed off on Alicia Boole Stott, who despite having no formal training made a significant contribution to the field of four-dimensional geometry. Born in Cork in 1860, she moved to London a few years after her father's sudden death in 1864.

Known informally as Alice, she received a general education, but like her sisters did not go on to attend university. All of the Boole sisters were successful in various different disciplines, but Alicia was the only one to show an exceptional aptitude for mathematics like her father. Her interest in four-dimensional thinking was sparked by her brother-in-law Charles Howard Hinton, who showed her some wooden geometric models when she was 18-years-old.

Alicia was fascinated and quickly realised she was able to understand and visualise four-dimensional shapes. Simply to satisfy her own curiosity, she worked out the six regular four-dimensional shapes she called 'polytopes', replicating work previously done by the Swiss mathematician Ludwig Schläfli that she was completely unaware of at the time. She also made cardboard models of the cross-sections of the polytopes she had visualised.

Alicia married Walter Stott and the couple had two children and she carried on with her normal life, forgetting about the fourth dimension for several years until her interest in the subject was reawakened by the work of the Dutch mathematician Pieter Schoute, who published a paper on the subject in 1895. Intrigued, Alicia sent Schoute pictures of the models she had built and he travelled to England to meet her. Suitably impressed, Schoute persuaded Alicia to publish her earlier work and collaborated with her on developing the ideas further.

She again ceased working on the subject however when Schoute died in 1913 but was awarded an honorary doctorate by Groningen University in 1914 in recognition of her contribution. Sixteen years later, her nephew introduced her to a young mathematician named Harold Scott MacDonald Coxete. The two began to work together on four-dimensional polytopes, leading to further discoveries published in a joint paper at Cambridge University. Boole Stott died in England in 1940 but interest in her work was revived again in 2001 when some of her original drawings were discovered in Groningen, and she was included in the 2007 book *Theory and History of Mathematical Models* by Irene Polo-Blanco.

ERNEST WALTON

Father of nuclear fission

The son of a Methodist minister born in the picturesque coastal town of Dungarvan in west Waterford, Ernest Thomas Sinton Walton is one of the most remarkable of all Irish scientists to date. He was a bright pupil and was especially gifted with science and maths, gaining a scholarship to Dublin's Trinity College in 1922 where he took mathematics and experimental science. In 1927 he went on to Cambridge University to work as a research scholar, where he gained his PhD under the guidance of Sir Ernest Rutherford at the Cavendish Laboratory. Walton began collaborating with John Cockcroft at the Cavendish Laboratory in the early 1930s and together they built a type of particle-accelerator and successfully managed to split the nuclei of lithium atoms by bombarding them with a stream of protons. It was the first time an atom had been split, and it was for this achievement that Walton and Cockcroft were awarded the Nobel Prize for physics in 1951.

Walton returned to Trinity College in Dublin where he was appointed Professor of Natural and Experimental Philosophy in 1946 and Senior Fellow in 1960. He died in 1995, aged 91, having donated his Nobel medal to Trinity College where he remained teaching for the rest of his career. The Walton Causeway Park in Dungarvan was dedicated to him in 1989. The Waterford Institute of Technology also named a new building after him, as did Methodist College Belfast.

CYNTHIA LONGFIELD

Dragonfly collector and famous entomologist

Known as 'Madame Dragonfly', Cork native Cynthia Longfield enjoyed an adventurous career as one of the leading entomologists of her generation. She was born in London in 1896, the daughter of Montifort and Alice Longfield, of Castlemary in Cloyne, East Cork. The youngest of three sisters, their family home was burned down during the Irish War of Independence in 1920 but was later rebuilt as Park House.

She joined the Army Service Corps in World War I and also worked in an aircraft factory. After the war she travelled extensively, exploring South America where she visited the Andes and Lake Titicaca. In 1923 she visited Egypt and reputedly caught a scorpion at the tomb of Ramses IX. Her career as an entomologist began to take off when later that year she joined an expedition to the Galapagos Islands and Pacific as an assistant to esteemed entymologist Cyril Collenette. The two set off into the jungle, using machetes to cut down the undergrowth and collecting specimens for the Natural History Museum in London.

In 1925 she became the first female member of the Entomological Society in London and joined the London Natural History Society in 1926, becoming its president in 1932. She also began working at the Natural History Museum in a voluntary capacity, cataloguing the Odonata (Dragonfly) grouping of insects that was under-researched at the time. In 1927 she travelled again, this time to Brazil's Mato Grosso state and returned to London with 38 specimens, including three that were previously unknown, one of which, Corphaeschna Longfieldae Kimmins was named after her.

She followed that with a journey to Southeast Asia in 1929 where she collected hundreds of specimens including butterflies and moths, discovering a new dragonfly species in the process, known as Agrionopter Insignis Cynthiae Lieftinck, which was also named in her honour. In the early 1930s she also visited Canada and Africa again, this time returning with six previously unknown species. On her return she continued cataloguing and publishing her findings and gave lectures on her expeditions. In 1937 she published *The Dragonflies of the British Isles*, which became the standard reference text on the Odonata order of insects. It was following the publication of this book that she earned the nickname "Madame Dragonfly" and the name stuck!

With the Second World War approaching Cynthia became one of the first women to join the Auxiliary Fire Service in 1938. Based at Brompton Fire Station near the Natural History Museum in London she took charge of 100 women and is said to have been responsible for saving the museum from destruction due to her quick thinking during a fire following an air raid.

After the war she continued to write and research and became an honorary associate of the Natural History Museum. She retired at 60 and in 1957 she returned to Castle Mary in Ireland where she lived until her death at the age of 96. She donated many specimens to the Royal Irish Academy as well as hundreds of books and records from her research. An exhibition of her life and work was held at the Royal Irish Academy in 2006.

IRELAND IN SPACE

Irish Americans have certainly played their part in the NASA space programme, with many of the early space pioneers having Irish heritage. The first man on the moon, Neil Armstrong, had roots in Fermanagh and Tyrone, while the family of his colleague Michael Collins hailed from County Cork. When it comes to astronauts, however, it is Irish American women in particular who have made the most impact.

KATHRYN DWYER SULLIVAN

Space trotter

Dr Kathryn Dwyer Sullivan was the first American female astronaut to walk in space, and a trailblazer for women in the American space programme. Her family came from the remote Beara Peninsula in Ireland's beautiful southwest where her grandfather, Denis "Lea" O'Sullivan, left the village of Lauragh for New York in 1893 eventually settling in California. Proud of her roots, Kathryn has visited her ancestral home, where she still has relatives living in the area.

She was born in Paterson, New Jersey in 1951 and raised in Los Angeles, California where she attended William Howard Taft High School in Woodland Hills. She went on to the University of California where she earned a BSc in Earth Sciences before completing a PhD in Geology at Dalhousie University in 1978. At Dalhousie she became involved with oceanographic survey expeditions.

In 1984 Sullivan joined NASA's space shuttle Challenger mission, where she made history by becoming the first female American astronaut to complete a space walk on October 11th; the first woman to do so was Russian Svetlana Savitskaya, who completed her first spacewalk on July 25th of the same year. Sullivan spent three and a half hours on the spacewalk with David Leestma during an eight-day shuttle mission completing 132 orbits of the Earth.

Sullivan returned to space in 1990 on the space shuttle Discovery, an important mission that launched the Hubble Space Telescope, a major leap forward for astronomy. Her final mission was aboard the space shuttle Atlantis in 1992, where she held the role of Payload Commander. This was the first Spacelab mission with the crew carrying out numerous experiments to help our understanding of the Earth's climate and atmosphere during its nine days. In total Dr Sullivan completed 532 hours in space over the three shuttle missions.

Back on Earth she joined the US Naval Reserve in 1988 as an oceanographer, a post she continued in until 2006. She was also president of the Center of Science and Industry (COSI), a major science centre in Columbus Ohio, as well as becoming Director of Ohio State University's Battelle Center for Mathematics. President George W. Bush appointed her to the National Science Board in 2004, and in 2009 she was elected chair of the General Interest in Science section of the American Association for the Advancement of Science. President Barack Obama appointed her Assistant Secretary of Commerce for Environmental Observation and Prediction and Deputy Administrator for the National Oceanic and Atmospheric Administration in 2011, and she became Under Secretary of Commerce for Oceans and Atmosphere in 2013.

With such a wide-ranging career in NASA, education, government and oceanography Dr Sullivan has been widely recognised for her contribution. She is a recipient of the Haley Space Flight Award, an Astronaut Hall of Fame inductee, recipient of the Adler Planetarium Women in Space Science Award and was awarded an honorary doctorate from Brown University.

Photo from the NASA [Public domain], via Wikimedia Commons.

NASA
KATHY
NASA

NASA

EILEEN MARIE COLLINS

First female space shuttle commander

Eileen Collin's parents both immigrated to the USA from County Cork and raised their four children in Elmira, New York. Eileen was born in 1956 and developed an early interest in flying and the burgeoning US space programme. She was schooled in Elmira before attending the nearby Corning Community College where she earned a degree in mathematics and science in 1976. She went on to Syracuse University where in 1978 she graduated with a BA in mathematics and economics. She then studied for a masters degree in operations research at Stanford University before completing her education with an MA in space systems operations management at Webster University in Missouri.

Following her degree from Syracuse, Collins joined the Air Force and was one of four women who were selected for pilot training at Vance Air Force Base in Oklahoma where she qualified as a pilot. Collins enjoyed a long and varied career as a pilot, flying a variety of aircraft and working as a pilot instructor. In 1986 she became an assistant professor in mathematics at the US Air Force Academy in Colorado and continued to fly. She was the second woman to attend the US Air Force Test Pilot School and was selected to join the astronaut programme in 1990.

Her first mission for NASA came in 1995 on the space shuttle Discovery, where she became the first woman to pilot the shuttle; the mission included the first rendezvous between a space shuttle and the Russian space station Mir. Her next mission was as pilot of the Atlantis in 1997 again on a rendezvous with Mir. In 1999 Collins became the first female commander of a space shuttle mission when she took charge of the Columbia's mission to deploy the Chandra X-Ray Observatory.

Her final mission was also as commander, this time of the shuttle Discovery in 2005. It was the first mission following the Columbia disaster in 2003, which resulted in the mission's crew being killed as the shuttle re-entered the Earth's atmosphere. Collins' 2005 mission to the International Space Station made her the first pilot to manoeuvre a shuttle through a 360-degree roll, which was done to enable astronauts on the space station to observe the underside of the shuttle to ensure there was no damage to it, which was the cause of the Columbia tragedy.

Collins has received multiple honours since retiring from her NASA career, including being inducted into the National Women's Hall Of Fame and the Astronaut Hall of Fame. The approach road to Syracuse Airport has been named after her and the New York State Legislature passed a resolution honouring her career. In Ireland she was conferred with an honorary Doctor of Science degree by University College Dublin.

Flying with Collins on her Columbia mission was Catherine Grace "Cady" Coleman. Coleman claims Irish heritage on both her maternal and paternal sides and has flown two space shuttle missions. With a background in chemistry she also spent time on the International Space Station. Coleman is a keen musician and flute player and brought with her to the space station a tin whistle from Paddy Maloney and a flute from Matt Molloy of the Chieftains! She is a member of Bandella, a band that includes fellow astronauts Chris Hadfield and Steven Robinson.

IRISH MEDICAL PIONEERS

The Irish have a long and proud history when it comes to the world of medicine and have made a huge contribution to health systems around the world. They have also been responsible for some major advances in medical technology that have changed the way medicine is practised today. Here are just a few of their stories.

JOHN JOLY

Radiotherapy pioneer

Offaly native, physicist and inventor John Joly is another Irishman whose work has had a lasting impact on the medical world. Joly is now remembered for developing radiotherapy treatment for cancer patients, as well as using radioactive decay to estimate the age of the earth and developing one of the first successful colour photography processes.

He was born in 1857 in Bracknagh, County Offaly and attended Trinity College Dublin, where he studied engineering. He had a distinguished academic career at Trinity and was appointed Professor of Geology and Mineralogy in 1897. Joly had a life-long interest in radiation and its possible practical applications. In 1913 he developed a technique to measure the radioactive decay of minerals with Sir Ernest Rutherford in Cambridge, from which they deduced the Devonian geological period began at least 400 million-years-ago. This was a major scientific breakthrough and laid the groundwork for subsequent studies of the age of the earth.

In 1914 he began working with Dr Walter Stevenson at Steven's Hospital in Dublin to investigate the potential use of radiation for treating cancer. He developed a technique for the extraction of radium (radon gas) to be used in cancer treatment that was then injected into the patient using a hollow needle. Joly was also a central figure in establishing the Royal Dublin Society's Radium Institute that supplied radium to hospitals for many years.

For his many accomplishments he was made a Fellow of the Royal Society in 1892 and was recognised with honorary degrees from the University of Cambridge, the National University of Ireland and the University of Michigan. Joly died in Dublin in December 1933 and is remembered through the Joly Memorial Lectures at the University of Dublin and a crater on Mars that was named after him in 1973.

Engraving of Steven's Hospital in Dublin 1780.

PHYLLIS CLINCH

Potato expert

No nation has more experience of the potential devastating impact of plant diseases than Ireland, and so it is perhaps appropriate that one of the world's most successful botanists in this area was Phyllis Clinch from Dublin. Born in 1901, she studied at University College Dublin (UCD) where she gained a first-class degree in botany and chemistry before going on to her masters in 1925, followed by a research fellowship with Dublin County Council. She obtained a PhD in plant physiology at Imperial College London in 1928.

Clinch completed her formal education studying cytology in Paris before being appointed an assistant to the Professor of Botany in Galway. She began her extensive career researching plant viruses here and then progressed to Albert Agricultural College in Dublin, where she became a research assistant in 1929 before joining the botany department in 1949 as a lecturer.

Clinch successfully identified damaging, symptomless viruses in potato plants and her findings were used as the basis for developing virus-free potato stocks. She also worked extensively on tomatoes and sugar beets, identifying degenerative diseases in the plants. Her research was widely published in many leading scientific journals including *Nature* and in 1943 she was awarded a Doctor of Science (DSc) in recognition of her work.

In 1949 she was one of the first women elected to the Royal Irish Academy, and in 1961 she was awarded the Boyle Medal by the Royal Dublin Society, the only woman to receive the award. The same year she became the first female Professor of Botany at UCD, a post she held until 1977 when she retired.

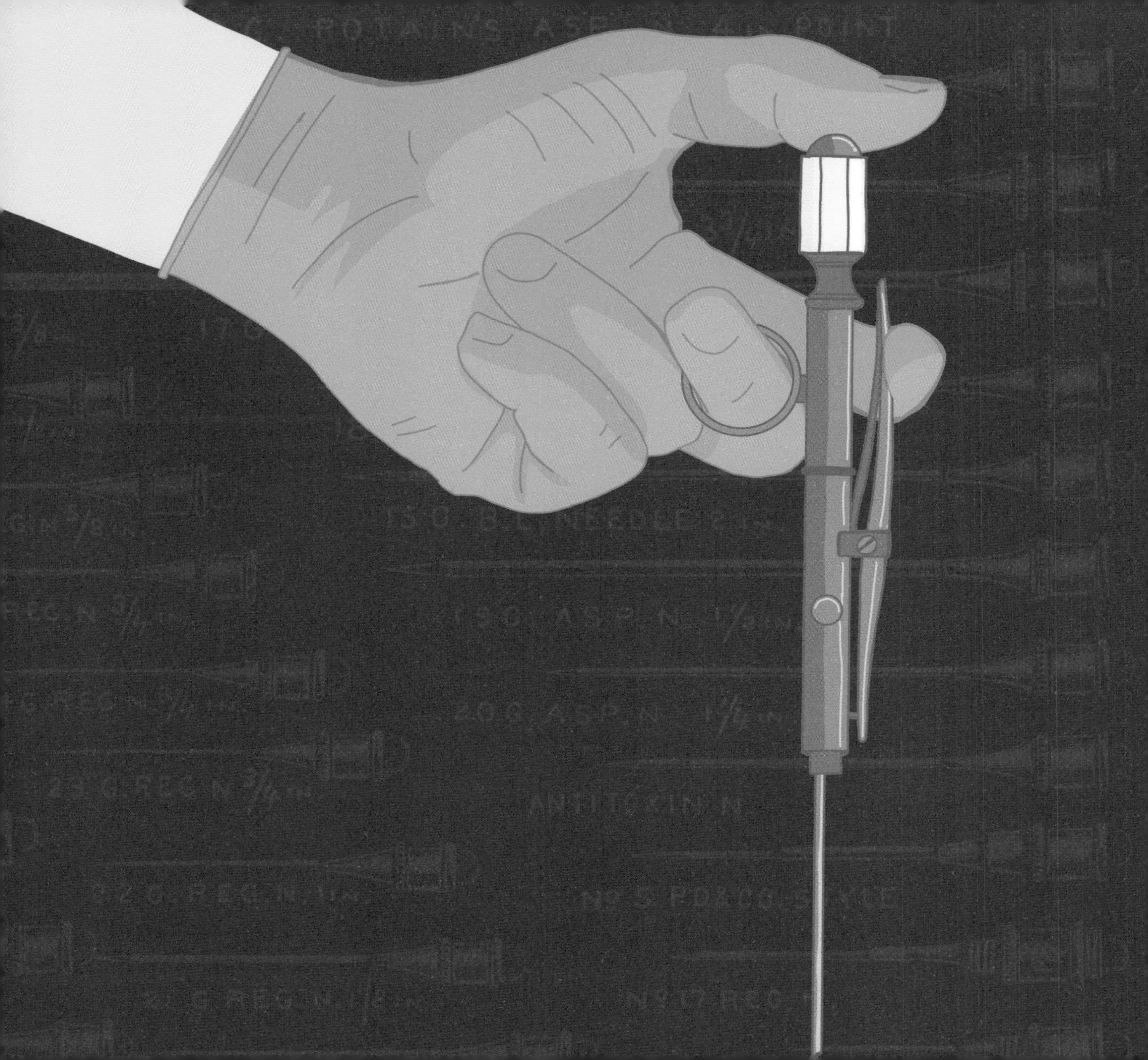

FRANCIS RYND

Sire of the hypodermic syringe

For many centuries the only way to effectively administer medicines to patients was orally or with the direct application to the skin of less successful remedies like leeches or fire. Though the idea of injecting directly into the tissue or bloodstream was recognised as far back as ancient Greece, the problem had always been finding an easy way to inject medicine into a patient.

The famous architect, Christopher Wren, made one of the first serious attempts in the 17th Century. Wren was also a scientist and mathematician, and while at Wadham College he carried out experiments injecting directly into the bloodstream of dogs using a hollow goose feather attached to an animal bladder! Although successful to a point, the obvious problems of infection that were not so well understood at the time meant that it was the last serious attempt for around 200 years.

It is at this stage that a doctor from Dublin enters the story: Francis Rynd. Born in 1801, Rynd came from a wealthy background in County Meath and was known as something of a playboy. He was, however, also a skilled surgeon and worked at Dublin's Meath Hospital, which was a leading centre for research in the 19th Century.

In 1844 Rynd was treating a patient with painful neuralgia in her face with the common treatment of the time, an orally administered morphine solution, but with little effect. He was aware that the specific nerves in the face were causing the problem and set about attempting to anaesthetise them directly. It was in tackling this problem that Rynd invented the hypodermic needle as a means of injecting morphine under the skin into the affected area.

He made his first syringe by using a small hollow tube known as a cannula and a cutting device known as a trocar. The small trocar was used to make the incision and then the morphine was fed into the tissue using gravity via the cannula, the first time such a procedure was ever carried out successfully on a human patient. The effect was immediate and Rynd's patient reported that she slept well for the first time in months following the procedure. The results were published in the *Dublin Medical Press* and Rynd's innovation quickly became widespread among his colleagues, leading to the rapid development of what would become known as the hypodermic syringe.

His idea was improved upon with the introduction of the glass syringe, a plunger mechanism and other modifications by Alexander Wood in Edinburgh, Charles Pravaz in Lyon and Charles Hunter in London. Charles Hunter was the first to describe the device as 'hypodermic', but it was Rynd's initial breakthrough that was the catalyst for its development. Rynd continued to use the technique throughout his medical career and died in Dublin in 1861.

Today the hypodermic syringe is an essential tool of modern medicine used for a huge range of applications from administering insulin for diabetics to taking blood samples, immunisation programmes and administering medicines and anaesthetics and it's all thanks to a simple innovation by a doctor from Dublin.

FRANK PANTRIDGE

Producer of the portable defibrillator

James Francis 'Frank' Pantridge was a remarkable man from Hillsborough in County Down. Born in 1916, Pantridge grew up on a farm and went to the Friend's School in Lisburn before going on to study medicine at Queens University in Belfast. Throughout his life he was known as something of a rebel and always questioned authority. He was expelled from school and clashed with faculty members during his university days. But he was also a brilliant student and graduated near the top of his year in 1939 and soon after was appointed as a house officer at Belfast's Royal Victoria Hospital.

His medical career was halted however by the outbreak of the Second World War, and Pantridge volunteered and was posted to Singapore. His experiences during the war had a defining impact on the rest of his life and he was eventually awarded the Military Cross for his service. Working as a medic on the frontline he witnessed the fall of the city to the Japanese and became a prisoner of war. Assigned to the infamous Burma Railway he was one of just a few hundred of the 7,000 prisoners of war to survive. During his time in Burma he contracted cardiac beriberi (a lack of thiamine that affects the cardiovascular system) and his health was seriously affected for the rest of his life.

Returning to Belfast, he resumed his medical career and developed an interest in cardiac medicine as a result of his own experiences. He studied at the University of Michigan under the renowned cardiologist Dr F.N. Wilson and returned to Belfast in 1950 where he set up a specialist cardiology unit at the Royal Victoria. At this unit he was instrumental in advancing European cardiac care, introducing modern CPR techniques and developing the innovation he is best remembered for: the world's first mobile defibrillator.

Pantridge was well aware that the first hour after a heart attack was vital to the patient's potential survival due to the onset of ventricular fibrillation, a major disruption of the heart's natural rhythm. If a short, severe electric shock was applied, the heart could be jolted back into its normal rhythm and mains-powered defibrillators were already in use in hospitals for this purpose. The problem was that by the time the patient made it to hospital, it was often already too late.

In 1965, Pantridge along with colleagues Alfred Mawhinney and John Geddes kitted out an ambulance with a defibrillator powered by car batteries and for the first time began bringing the defibrillator to the patient. He was convinced that the idea could be developed to produce a truly portable version, and this proved to be the case. Many in the British medical establishment met his innovation with scepticism, but in the US it was a different story and mobile defibrillators began to be adopted across the country. In time his idea was accepted and developed across the world, and today he is often referred to as the father of emergency medicine. A statue of Pantridge honouring his contribution was unveiled in Lisburn by his friend, Irish rugby hero Jack Kyle, in 2006.

VINCENT BARRY

Leprosy specialist

Of all communicable diseases, leprosy has long been one of the most feared and one of the most misunderstood. It has been recorded for thousands of years and for much of history those suffering from the disease have been banished to leper colonies to live apart from the rest of society. Leprosy was first thought to be a hereditary condition but was proven to be a bacterial infection by the Norwegian scientist G. H. Hansen in 1873. After a long incubation period (often years) leprosy presents itself through lesions and marks on the skin and eyes, affects nerve endings leading to loss of feeling and can affect the respiratory system and lead to general weakness in the patient. It is often incorrectly seen as a highly contagious disease when in fact the likelihood of contagion is very low, but it was this fear of contagion that often led sufferers to be ostracised from their communities in 'leper colonies'.

In the first half of the 20th Century, leprosy and the related disease tuberculosis were rampant across the world, but tackling the more deadly TB became a priority for medical researchers. Leading a small team at Trinity College in Dublin attempting to cure the disease was Vincent Christopher Barry. Barry was an unassuming man, the youngest of 11 children who grew up in Sunday's Well in Cork city. Born in 1908, he won a scholarship to University College Dublin where he studied organic chemistry before moving to Galway to work in research. After more than ten years in the west of Ireland he moved with his family to Dublin to take a job at the Medical Research Council. Initially developing drugs to combat TB, his team also began to look at possible uses for their research in combating leprosy.

He visited a leper colony in India to see for himself the realities of dealing with the disease and returned to Dublin determined to help its sufferers. In 1954, Barry led a team that was able to synthesise a compound called B663, known as Clofazimine, which would become a crucial part of the multi-drug treatment now used for leprosy around the world. It was introduced by the Indian government in the 1970s and by 1981 became mandatory for the treatment of leprosy by the World Health Organisation (WHO); it is also on the WHO's 'List of Essential Medicines', a list of the 'most important medication needed in a basic health system'.

Barry died in 1975 in the knowledge that his discovery had already changed the lives of tens of thousands of people and would help millions more in the future. In recognition of their vital work Barry and his team were awarded the UNESCO Science Prize in 1980.

IRELAND'S COMPUTER GENIUSES

Modern Ireland is home to many of the world's biggest international information technology and computing companies, with the likes of Apple, Google, Facebook and Intel all having offices in the country. Ireland itself has also produced award-winning technological innovators and inventors that have contributed greatly to the advancement of modern computing.

GEORGE BOOLE

Mathematical genius

George Boole made one of the most significant developments in mathematics that paved the way for the modern information technology industry while at Queens College in Cork, in the mid-19th Century. Boole was a self-taught mathematician and was appointed to his position in Cork with little real academic experience, something that would be unheard of today. Born in Lincoln in England in 1815, his remarkable talent paved the way for much of the mathematic basis of the modern information age, from electronics to the Internet and World Wide Web.

Acknowledged as the father of pure mathematics, he came to Ireland in 1849 having been appointed the first professor of mathematics at the new Queen's College Cork, now University College Cork. He was the son of a Lincoln shoemaker and did not attend university himself, but worked as a teacher in the north of England and studied mathematics in his spare time. He began studying algebra and calculus and also started to publish his own research in the 1830s, which gained him recognition in academic circles.

It was this experience that enabled him to successfully apply for the new professor's position in Cork and soon after arriving he met his wife Mary Everest in 1850; she would later go on to become a mathematics teacher herself. Boole's greatest contribution to the field of mathematics was the development of 'Boolean algebra', a system he devised for representing logical questions in mathematical form using '1s' and '0s' instead of numbers. The breakthrough had massive implications for the future of mathematics, electronics and information technology and was essential to the development of digital technology and computer programming.

Boole published his most significant work, *An Investigation of the Laws of Thought*, in 1854. He was elected to the Royal Society in 1857 and was awarded honorary degrees from the universities of Oxford and Dublin in recognition of his work. Boole died, aged just 49, in 1864 after contracting pneumonia. Reportedly already suffering from lung problems, he had walked the three miles in the rain from his home in the suburb of Ballintemple to give a lecture at the college, which he did, still wearing his wet clothes. Soon afterwards he became ill and never recovered. Boole is now remembered as one of the most important figures in the history of mathematics. A crater on the Moon is named in his honour and he is remembered at his old college through the Boole Library and a fine stained-glass window that was erected after his death. In 2015, the year of his bicentenary, a major programme of events was held at UCC to honour his legacy.

KAY MCNULTY MAUCHLY ANTONELLI

War-time programming pioneer

Born at the height of the Irish War of Independence in Creeslough, County Donegal, Kathleen (Kay) McNulty was the daughter of an IRA man, James McNulty. On the very day she was born, February 12th 1921, Kay's father was arrested and sent to prison in Derry for his activities in the war. He was released two years later and soon afterwards emigrated with his family to Philadelphia in the United States. James established a successful masonry business there and Kay attended the Hallahan Catholic Girls High School in Philadelphia, where she showed a natural ability for mathematics.

She went on to study at the Chestnut Hill College for Women and graduated in 1942 with a degree in mathematics, one of only three women in a class of 92 to do so. Not wanting to become a teacher, she sought out job opportunities where she could use her qualifications and secured a place at the Moore School of Electrical Engineering at the University of Pennsylvania. With the war in full swing her job entailed calculating the trajectories for artillery firing tables, a time-consuming but extremely important role.

Kay proved to be an excellent 'computer' and within a few months she was assigned to work on the differential analyser, which at the time was among the most powerful analogue computers in the world. She once again proved herself to be highly capable at the complex work and was chosen to be part of the team to work on the newly developed ENIAC (Electronic Numerical Integrator And Computer), the world's first electronic general-purpose computer, a top secret project of the US military. The new computer was able to carry out, in seconds, calculations that by hand would take 40 hours or more. The machine had no memory however, and no manual, so Kay and her colleagues had to programme every instruction.

After the war the machine was moved to the US Army proving grounds in Aberdeen, Maryland and Kay continued working on the project. In 1948 she married the co-inventor of the ENIAC John Mauchly. She dedicated the next years of her life to raising a family in Pennsylvania but continued to maintain her interest in computing technology.

John went on to found one of the world's first commercial computing companies, and Kay helped her husband with his designs both for hardware, software and in developing programming languages. In 1980 John died and Kay began to look for recognition for his role in the development of computing, giving several interviews and attending conferences and lectures on the subject. She married photographer Severo Antonelli in 1985.

In 1997 she was inducted into the Women In Technology International (WITI) Hall of Fame and she also took part in a documentary about the ENIAC project and its influence. In her native Donegal, the Letterkenny Institute ofTechnology established the annual Kay McNulty medal and prize for the best computer science student in her memory, and in 2016 Dublin City University re-named their computer science building in her honour.

IRELAND IN THE MINES

The 19th Century was an exciting time for mining as the Industrial Revolution spread from Britain to Europe and America, the age of steam, iron and steel demanding ever-greater resources to fire the furnaces and move the trains. Ireland, with little resources of its own, had only a small mining heritage. However, several Irishmen and women played their part in the new industry, from Germany's industrial heartland to the wilds of Butte Montana and the gold rushes of the American West to seek their fortune and develop their careers.

JOHN MACKAY

The Bonanza King

Born in Dublin in 1831, John Mackay would become one of the richest men in the world thanks to his involvement in mining the Comstock Lode, a huge silver deposit discovered in a remote Nevada Mountainside in 1859. Mackay immigrated to New York with his family in 1840 when he was nine-years-old, but always took pride in his Irish roots. He initially trained as a shipyard worker but headed west in the 1850s to take part in the California Gold Rush and seek his fortune. He was moderately successful in California but missed the height of the boom in 1859 when a new strike, this time silver, was reported in Nevada to the east.

The Comstock Lode, as it was known, was a large silver deposit found on Mount Davidson in northern Nevada, in what was then the Utah Territory, and was the first major silver discovery in the USA. As with the California Gold Rush, thousands of prospectors flocked to the area, but this time John Mackay was there at the start. He developed a reputation as hardworking and fair-minded and was appointed as a supervisor with the Caledonia Tunnel and Mining Company, gradually working his way up in the tough frontier community that became known as Virginia City.

Mackay then entered into a partnership with three other Irishmen: William O'Brien, James Flood and James Fair, who together would become known as 'The Bonanza Firm'. In 1873 the four discovered a major new deposit known as the 'Big Bonanza' that would ensure vast wealth for them all, particularly Mackay, who was the biggest shareholder. Before the discovery Mackay had already become a wealthy man working diligently on other prospects and investing what he made wisely.

The scope of his further investments changed dramatically when the four founded the Bank of Nevada, after which Mackay became involved in the communications business. In 1884 he formed the Commercial Cable Company and laid two transatlantic telegraph cables connecting to Waterville in his native Ireland, sparking a price war with Western Union who previously held a monopoly; he also established a domestic network. Next he focussed on the Pacific and with the Commercial Pacific Cable Company began connecting California with Hawaii, the Philippines and China. He did not live to see this final project come to fruition but its completion was overseen by his son Clarence, who led the communications business for many years.

Mackay was well known for his philanthropy, funding several Catholic charities and was respected as a good employer by his workers. He died in London in 1902 at the age of 70 and his body was returned to the USA and buried in Green-Wood Cemetery, Brooklyn. After his death, his family donated the Mackay School of Mines building to the University of Nevada at its Reno Campus in 1908, where a statue by the famous sculptor Gutzon Borglum of Mount Rushmore fame is dedicated to his memory.

Alta mine mill and dump on Gold Hill, Comstock Lode, 1896.

WILLIAM THOMAS MULVANY

German miner

William Thomas Mulvany was born in 1806 to a middle-class Catholic family in Sandymount, Dublin. He studied engineering and decided to convert to the Church of Ireland to improve his chances of finding work in the civil service. He joined the Ordnance Survey Office and later the Board of Public Works, working on several drainage schemes and was involved in the construction of the Shannon-Erne canal which gave him experience in drainage and reclamation.

In 1854 he visited the Low Countries and the Ruhr region in western Germany; the areas were rapidly industrialising at the time and geological surveys had shown them to be rich in coal deposits. The south of the Ruhr was already being exploited, but Mulvany saw an opportunity in the north, which had been deemed by local engineers as too boggy and inaccessible. Mulvany was among the first to see the full potential of the area as one of the world's most productive coal regions, and when the industry was deregulated he seized the opportunity.

Mulvany formed a consortium to buy underperforming mines in Gelsenkirchen and opened a new mine he named 'Hibernia', with excavations beginning on St Patrick's Day 1855; he also bought mines in nearby Herne that he renamed 'Shamrock'. By 1864 Mulvany's mines were producing more than 300,000 tonnes of coal a year and employing more than 1,000 people. The Ruhr was transformed into an industrial powerhouse and is to this day Germany's industrial heartland.

Mulvany's impact on the area was not forgotten, and he was made an honorary citizen of Gelsenkirchen in 1880. In Gelsenkirchen, the town's Mulvanystraße is named in his honour, while Herne has Shamrockstraße commemorating the mine he operated in the area.

NELLIE CASHMAN

Frontierswoman

Ellen 'Nellie' Cashman was a prospector, philanthropist, businesswoman and adventurer who made her mark in the man's world of the Old West. She was born in 1845 in Midleton, East Cork and immigrated to America in 1850 with her sister and mother following the death of her father Patrick. They first settled in Boston before moving to San Francisco in 1865. Ellen became known as Nellie and the name stuck for the rest of her life.

By 1872 she established a boarding house in Pioche, Nevada, a remote silver-mining outpost. Pioche had a reputation as one of the toughest towns in America, where gunfights and Indian raids were common, but Nellie was not deterred and became involved in the Catholic Church in the area, which she would remain a strong supporter of for the rest of her life. While in Pioche, Nellie began to learn more about mining and prospecting and became very knowledgeable on the subjects.

She next headed to the Cassiar Mountains in the far north of British Columbia in Canada. This was a very remote and inhospitable area that was attracting an influx of adventurous prospectors, but it was a tough place to survive. In 1873 a group of miners became stranded at a remote camp in the area and Nellie organised a rescue party to get help and supplies to the men. She led the rescue team for an incredible 77 days in the harsh conditions despite being warned it was too dangerous by the Canadian Army. The mission was a success, however, and the miners numbering somewhere between 25 and 75 were saved thanks to her efforts. Following the expedition, Cashman was given the nickname 'Angel of the Cassiar'.

In the 1880s she lived in the famous mining town of Tombstone, Arizona where she operated another boarding house and restaurant and became a pillar of the local community. She fundraised for the construction of the Sacred Heart Church in the town and managed to persuade the owners of the Crystal Palace Saloon (who included Wyatt Earp) to host Sunday services until the church was finished. She was a strong supporter of local charities like the Red Cross and was active in helping those who had fallen on hard times.

While in Tombstone she also took a stand against a public execution of four men who were involved in a bank robbery – Nellie tore down the grandstand erected for the 'event' and the sentences were carried out in private. She also saved a mine owner from an angry mob during a labour dispute, and took in her sister's five children after their mother's untimely death.

She continued her prospecting travelling to various parts of North America, often establishing businesses where she went and continuing to donate to charities. In 1897 she moved to Alaska as the Klondike gold rush got underway, living in Koyukuk and Fairbanks. She spent the last 20 years of her life in the area and once again became a pillar of the community, fundraising for the church, local hospitals and charities. She also became a champion female musher (dog sledder) at the age of 79! A memorial was erected in her honour in Midleton, County Cork in 2015 and she was also inducted into the Alaska Mining Hall of Fame.

Anaconda Copper Mining Company.

MARCUS DALY

The Copper King

Another Irishman who would become a giant of the American mining industry, this time in copper, was Marcus Daly. He came from a poor farming background in the townland of Derrylea, near Ballyjamesduff in County Cavan. Born in 1841, the youngest of 11 children, at the age of 15 Daly left Cavan for America. He landed in New York City and scraped by doing menial jobs until he had saved enough money to head west to opportunity. Daly travelled to the boomtown of San Francisco and again took on various unskilled jobs before heading to the Comstock Lode like so many other Irish to try his luck at mining.

Daly got work at Comstock with John Mackay and was a quick learner. In Virginia City he also met George Hearst, the father of the future newspaper baron William Randolph, and Lloyd Tevis. Tevis and Hearst owned a mine at Ophir, Utah and by 1871 Daly was working there as a supervisor for the Walker Brothers of Salt Lake City. Daly gained a detailed knowledge of the prospects in the area and advised Hearst and his backers to buy the Ontario mine east of Salt Lake City; they took his advice and it delivered huge profits for the investors.

In 1876 Daly travelled to Bute, Montana, again in search of silver for the Walker Brothers. They purchased the Alice mine and Daly ran it for them, receiving a small share. It was while working at the Alice mine that he began to come across large deposits of copper. He made wider investigations and was soon convinced that Bute was sitting on top of an enormous deposit of copper. Copper was becoming a highly valuable commodity, needed for the new technology of electricity and for telegraph cables of the type being laid across the oceans by John Mackay. He tried to persuade the Walkers to buy up the land to exploit the copper but they were not convinced. Daly sold his share in the Alice mine and bought his own prospect to the west with the help of Hearst and Tevis, known as the Anaconda. At first, they hit silver again, but it was what was underneath that would make Marcus Daly his fortune, a massive copper deposit worth millions of dollars.

The problem with copper was the cost of smelting it; because there were no facilities in North America to do it, the ore had to be sent all the way to South Wales for smelting, which made it prohibitively expensive. The size of the deposit at Anaconda changed the game, however, since it was big enough that Daly was able to justify building a smelter right there. The town of Anaconda was also built to house the workers for the mine and smelter. Within ten years the mine was producing more than $15 million dollars' worth of copper a year.

Daly became enormously rich and made a myriad of investments including a railroad, timber forests, a newspaper and banks. He built a mansion and ranch by the Bitterroot River south of Missoula where he indulged his passion for breeding racehorses. He also remembered his roots in Cavan and donated money for the construction of a new church, St Mary's at Crosserlough, not far from his childhood home. One of the richest men in America, he died at the age of 58 in New York City. A statue of Daly was erected at the Montana School of Mines, now Montana Tech, in Bute; in 1929 in Hamilton, near his home in the Bitterroot Valley, The Marcus Daly Memorial Hospital was named in his memory.

THE IRISH IN AMERICA

Irish immigrants were integral to the construction of modern-day America. The massive wave of Irish emigration in the 19th Century following the Great Famine saw hundreds of thousands leave the island in search of work and a better life, making a huge impact around the world, including the USA. These immigrants helped build canals, plan cities, construct transportation infrastructure - in short, their work and toil built the very foundations of one of the world's most powerful nations.

JOHN B. MCDONALD

Subway strategist

In the late 19th Century Lower Manhattan became more and more crowded and it was clear that a more radical solution would be needed for the city's transport needs: a subway. The man for the job was one John B. McDonald from Fermoy in County Cork. McDonald was a successful engineering contractor and had recently finished the Howard Street Tunnel in Baltimore a major railway project that had taken more than four years to complete. This experience was enough to secure him the job of developing New York's first subway system, the tunnels for which would be dug by Irish workers. The contract was awarded in 1900 and McDonald set about subcontracting for the massive project that was completed in less than four years at a cost of about $40 million.

The new IRT system was 20 miles long and included 48 stations, 33 of which were underground. The New York subway would grow from McDonald's initial system to become one of the longest and busiest metros in the world and would prove vital for the development of New York City itself. McDonald died in 1911 just six years after his IRT line opened for business; as a mark of respect the entire subway system stopped running for two minutes in his honour.

New York City Subway Map. Created by CountZ via Wikimedia Commons.

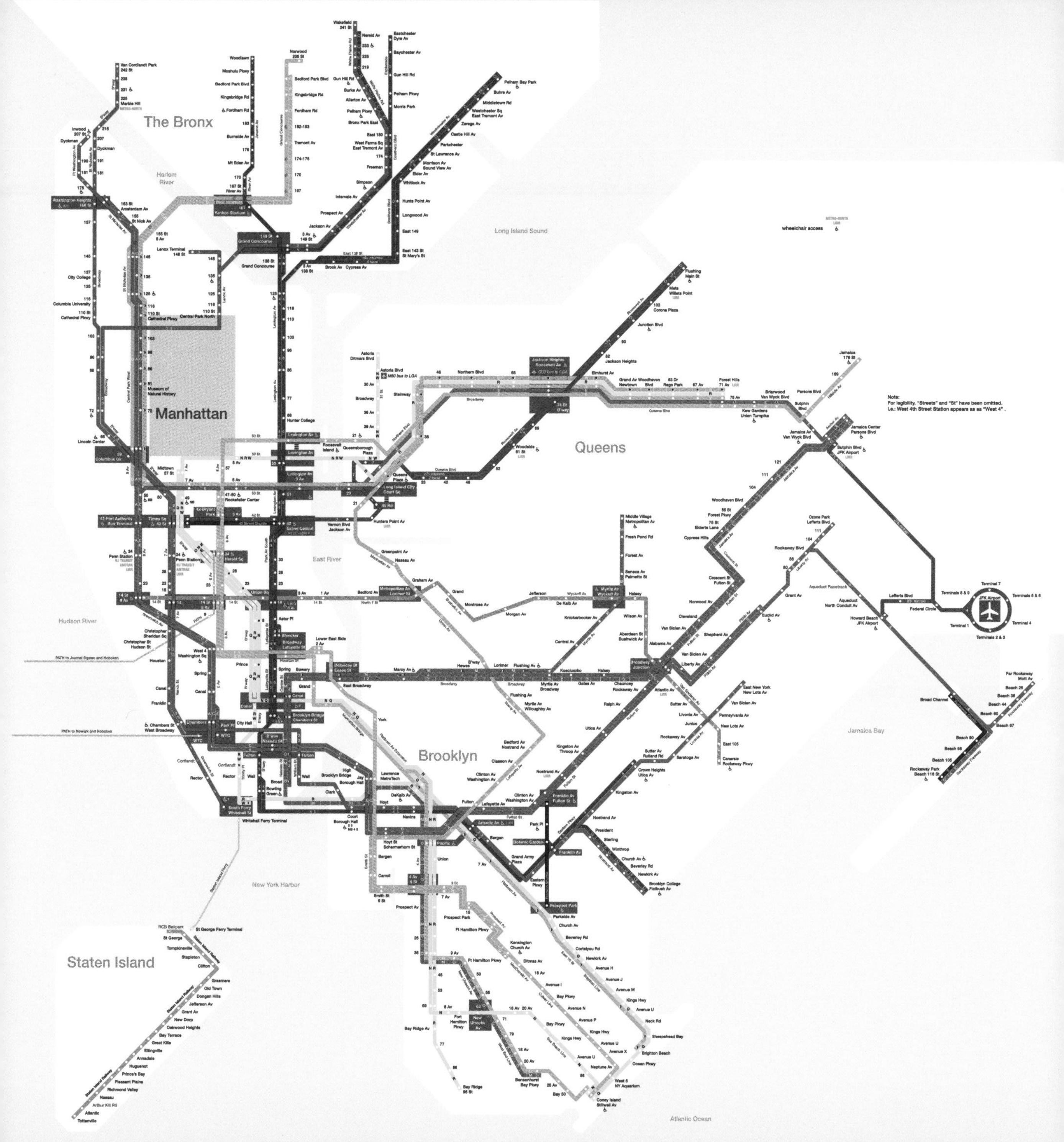

Note:
For legibility, "Streets" and "St" have been omitted.
i.e.: West 4th Street Station appears as as "West 4".
wheelchair access
The Bronx
Manhattan
Queens
Brooklyn
Staten Island
Harlem River
Hudson River
East River
Long Island Sound
New York Harbor
Jamaica Bay
Atlantic Ocean
JFK Airport
PATH to Journal Square and Hoboken
PATH to Newark and Hoboken
Staten Island Ferry
Whitehall Ferry Terminal
St George Ferry Terminal

JOHN STEPHENSON

Streetcar creator

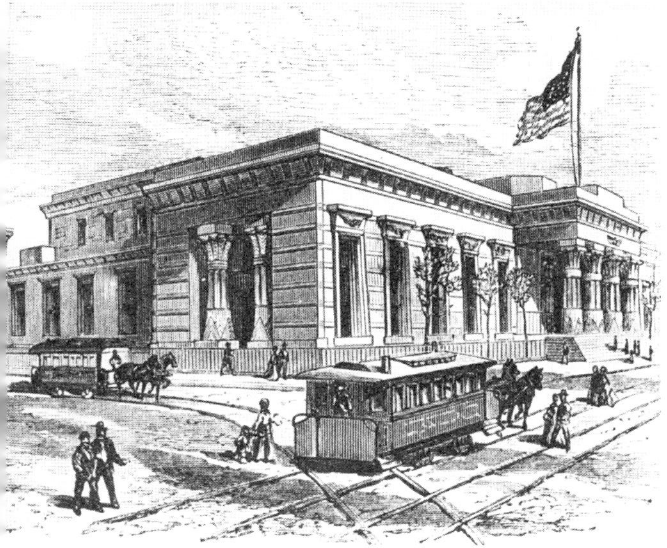

Streetcars in New York in 1870.

New York was founded by the Dutch as New Amsterdam in the early 17th Century and had grown steadily as a colonial outpost, becoming a major trading town of British America. After independence, New York's growth began to accelerate and by the mid-19th Century it had already become a major city. Millions of emigrants arrived from Europe throughout the 19th Century and by 1850 it is estimated there were some 200,000 Irish in New York, almost a quarter of the population.

The first streetcars in the world were developed in New York by one such Irishman by the name of John Stephenson, who was born in Armagh in 1809. Stephenson started his own company in 1831 building coaches and horse-drawn omnibuses and developed the world's first omnibuses to run on rails (streetcars) between The Bowery and Fourth Avenue. He was also responsible for developing the first railway in New York, the New York and Harlem Railroad that initially used horses but gradually developed to a steam and then electric railway in the 1850s, it is now part of the Metro-North commuter rail system. Stephenson's company was very successful in its heyday selling streetcars to cities around the world.

JOHN MCSHAIN

Architect of Washington

Responsible for constructing many of the major public buildings in Washington D.C. during the 20th Century, Irish-American John McShain became known as 'the man who built Washington'. His father, John McShane Senior, emigrated to the United States from Derry in 1860 and settled in Philadelphia where his brother had already established a building firm. In 1888 John set up his own successful contracting company. The spelling of the family name is said to have changed from McShane to McShain due to an administrative error in 1900.

John Junior was born in Philadelphia in 1896 and his parents were able to send him to La Salle University. Not long after graduating he was faced with taking over the family building firm in 1919 following his father's death. McShain proved to be an exceptional businessman and grew the firm to become one of the largest building contractors on the east coast. The company became one of the leading contractors in the Washington DC area.

McShain's company were the lead contractor for many of the large government schemes built in the following years, working on more than 100 projects including the refurbishment of the White House, the Pentagon, the Jefferson Memorial, Washington National Airport and the JFK Center for the Performing Arts. McShain's success brought him great wealth and he invested in thoroughbred racehorses in the USA and Ireland, winning several major races including the Irish Derby, Goodwood, Ascot, the St Leger and the Prix de l'Arc de Triomphe.

John and his wife Mary Horstmann were regular visitors to Ireland and in 1956 they bought Kenmare House in Killarney, County Kerry as part of a consortium and took full ownership of the house and grounds in 1959. The property included Ross Castle and Innisfallen Island, the site of an early Christian monastery. They refurbished the property, renaming it Killarney House and retired there in 1959. In 1973 he donated Innisfallen Island to the Irish State and in 1978 he sold most of the land he owned in the area to the Irish government at a reduced price on the assurance it would be incorporated into Killarney National Park. The building was opened to the public in July 2017 as a new interpretative centre for the Killarney National Park.

WILLIAM MULHOLLAND

Water wizard

Located in an arid basin between the mountains and the Pacific Ocean, the city of Los Angeles really shouldn't exist, since it lacks the most vital resource needed for any settlement: water. The fact that modern Los Angeles is a sprawling metropolis of more than 12 million people, home to the world's entertainment industry, a former oil boomtown and the second city of the USA is largely down to the work of a daring Irish engineer named William Mulholland.

Mulholland was born in Belfast in 1855, the son of Dubliners Hugh and Ellen Mulholland. When he was still a small child the family returned to their native Dublin. He attended the Christian Brothers in Dublin and at the age of 15 he left home to join the Merchant Navy, spending the next few years working as a merchant seaman on the transatlantic routes between Britain and America before leaving the service in the 1870s to settle in the USA.

He arrived in the small city of Los Angeles in 1877; at that time the population was less than 10,000, though LA was already experiencing significant growth as people attracted by the California Gold Rush looked for new opportunities and a place to settle down. Mulholland's early days in LA were spent doing various manual jobs whenever he could get them, including gold prospecting and digging wells. He eventually secured a job with the Los Angeles City Water Company (LACWC) under the supervision of Frederick Eaton, who hired him as a supervisor on the city's main water supply conduit, the Zanja Madre. The post was known as a 'zanjero', and it was his first step in what would be a remarkable career.

Mulholland had only a basic formal education but continually sought to improve his knowledge and was a voracious reader on subjects like mathematics, engineering and literature. He impressed Eaton with his hard work and dedication, and was soon promoted within the ranks of the water company. In 1880 he was given the responsibility of installing the first iron water pipeline in Los Angeles.

In 1898 Eaton ran for mayor and promised voters he would build a new water system for Los Angeles if he were elected; the city's lack of an adequate water supply was already a major issue and was hindering potential growth. Eaton was elected and one of his first acts as mayor was to create the Los Angeles Water Department, and he made Mulholland its chief engineer. Mulholland was now ready to tackle the water shortage in LA and set to work.

With no natural water supply available anywhere near the city, Eaton and Mulholland had to look to the state's interior for a viable water source, and they identified the Owens Valley some 250 miles north of the city as the best option. Although the challenge of getting water to LA would be huge, there was also another problem: most of the land needed to build the aqueduct was privately owned by farmers who relied on the very water supply Eaton and Mulholland wanted to divert to the city.

Eaton was an experienced developer and set about purchasing land for the aqueduct; he simply didn't tell the farmers in the area what he was planning. Nevertheless, Eaton continued with his efforts for several years until in 1905 the necessary land had been assembled. Mulholland was made chief

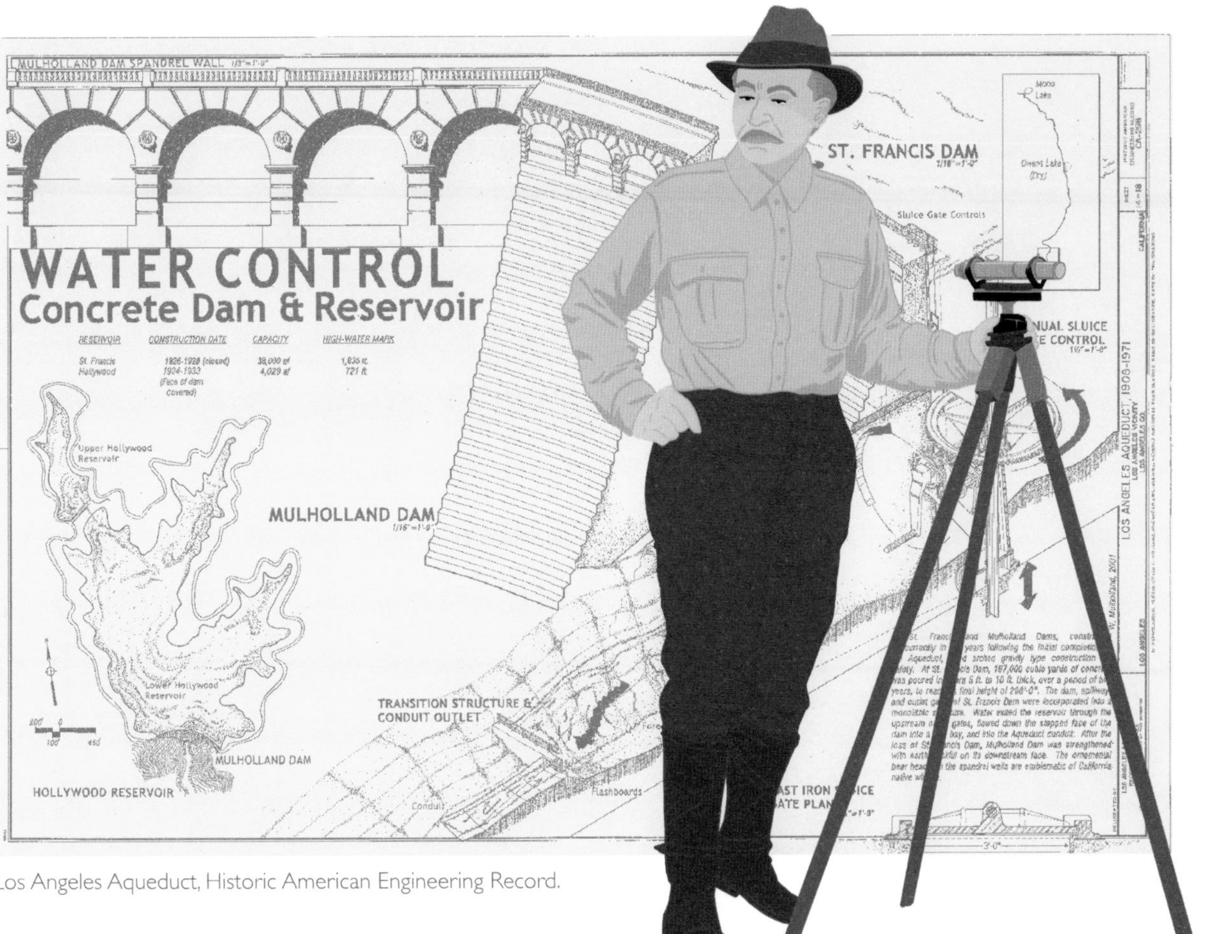

Los Angeles Aqueduct, Historic American Engineering Record.

engineer of what became known as the Los Angeles Aqueduct in 1906 and construction began almost immediately. It was one of the biggest civil engineering projects ever undertaken in America, employing up to 5,000 men and 6,000 mules and extending more than 220 miles, including 142 tunnels. The project was completed in 1913 and at the opening ceremony Mulholland famously told the assembled crowds of more than 30,000, "There it is. Take it".

He is remembered by the famous Mulholland Drive in Los Angeles, the scenic route along the spine of the Hollywood Hills that is named after him as well as the William Mulholland Memorial Fountain located at the south end of Griffith Park; but the most fitting memorial is the Los Angeles Aqueduct that to this day provides water to half of the city of Los Angeles.

JAMES HOBAN

White House visionary

Among the world's most recognisable buildings and voted America's second favourite building in an American Institute of Architects poll in 2007 (the Empire State Building came first), the White House in Washington D.C. was inspired by an Irish building, and designed and built by Irish architect James Hoban.

Hoban was born into a tenant farming family in Cuffesgrange, located between the town of Callan and Kilkenny city in 1758. By his early 20s he was an accomplished carpenter. He gained a place at the Dublin Society to study architectural drawing, where he excelled and went on to work with teacher James Ivory, recognised as one of the leading lights of Georgian architecture in Dublin. Under Ivory's guidance the young Hoban gained experience and expertise, and in 1785 decided to immigrate to America to find his fortune as an architect in the New World.

Hoban arrived at a time of chaos and instability in America, with the fledgling nation still trying to assert its independence. After a stint in Philadelphia he moved to Charleston, South Carolina where he designed the Charleston County Courthouse (1790). It's thought that Hoban may have met America's first president George Washington in 1791 in Charleston when Washington was conducting his southern tour and admired Hoban's work.

At Washington's suggestion he travelled to the nation's temporary capital in Philadelphia in 1792 to enter the design competition for the president's official residence. The inspiration for Hoban's classical design was Dublin's Leinster House. The simple design suited the new administration, which didn't want the kind of 'palatial' building that might appeal to European monarchs, and Hoban's design was chosen as the winner. Hoban supervised the construction of the building, which was completed in 1801.

It was always Washington's intention that the building be easily adapted and expanded for future generations, saying that it should be of use "beyond the present day" as indeed it proved to be. Another war with Britain erupted in 1812 and in 1814 the old colonial masters occupied Washington and almost completely destroyed the White House along with the new Capitol building a few blocks away. The superstructure survived however and when hostilities ceased it was Hoban who was called on to supervise its reconstruction in early 1815.

As well as designing the White House, Hoban was one of the supervising architects for the new U.S. Capitol building completed in 1800 and he has left an indelible mark on the architecture of the nation's capital city being involved in the construction of the U.S. Treasury building and several other government buildings in Washington. He spent the rest of his life living in Washington, teaching and working on several public projects. In 2008 to mark the 250th anniversary of his birth a memorial was unveiled near the site of his birth in County Kilkenny designed by architecture students from the Catholic University of Washington D.C. but his lasting legacy is of course the White House itself.

Daguerrotype of the south front of the White House, 1846.

MICHAEL MAURICE O'SHAUGHNESSY

Dam extraordinaire

Of all the engineers who have been responsible for building the modern city of San Francisco, among the most influential was Irishman Michael Maurice O'Shaughnessy. Born in County Limerick in 1864, O'Shaughnessy studied in Cork, Dublin and Galway before graduating as an engineer in 1884. He travelled to London in search of work but was unable to secure a job so he decided to head to America instead. He sailed to New York and then took a train to the West Coast, arriving in San Francisco in 1885.

In California O'Shaughnessy worked for the Sierra Valley Railroad and then the Southern Pacific Railroad where he was part of a team that planned the towns of Mill Valley and Sausalito. He opened his own successful consulting firm in San Francisco in 1889 and was appointed Chief Engineer for the city of San Francisco in 1912 by Mayor James Rolph; O'Shaughnessy had to be persuaded to take the position by his wife as the city had not always paid him in the past and he would have to take a pay cut! San Francisco had suffered a devastating earthquake and fire in 1906 and the disaster presented O'Shaughnessy with an opportunity to modernise the city's infrastructure and plan for future growth.

Among the major projects completed under his supervision were the Twin Peaks and Stockton Street tunnels, the Twin Peaks Reservoir, the Municipal Railway system, the streetcar system, a pressurised fire hydrant network as well as several major sewers, streets and roadways. He is best remembered, however, for the controversial Hetch Hetchy Dam project. With San Francisco growing at a rapid rate it was clear that the current water supply would be eventually be unable to supply the growing population. With no sufficient freshwater supply nearby O'Shaughnessy had to look east to the interior of the state to find a viable solution.

His answer was found in the Hetch Hetchy Valley, a scenic, unspoiled valley in the Yosemite National Park more than 150 miles away. The decision proved controversial from the beginning but plans were drawn up to dam the Tuolumne River in the Sierra Mountains and link the supply to San Francisco through a major network of pipes, tunnels, pumping stations and reservoirs. The plans were vetoed by President Theodore Roosevelt, who was a strong supporter of the national parks, but were eventually given the go-ahead by his successor, Woodrow Wilson in 1913. Construction began in 1919 and was completed in 1923 but delays and problems meant that the dam did not begin supplying the city until 1934. O'Shaughnessy ceased working on the project in 1932 when the newly formed Public Utilities Commission took over the works. The dam was named the O'Shaughnessy Dam in his memory and O'Shaughnessy Boulevard in San Francisco was named after him.

JASPER O'FARRELL

San Francisco developer

While the east coast of North America saw rapid growth in the early part of the 19th Century, things moved more slowly over on the west coast. California was at that time one of the world's most remote regions, difficult to get to by land or sea and mostly undeveloped until the Gold Rush of 1849. Originally a Spanish colony, it became part of Mexico and was ceded to the United States in the Treaty of Guadalupe Hidalgo in 1848; California did not become a state until 1850.

In the early days San Francisco was by far the most important settlement on the West Coast since it was the only major port, and it became a boomtown during the Gold Rush. Irishman Jasper O'Farrell helped to make the city what it is today.

Wexford native O'Farrell led an extraordinary life of adventure in the New World and was instrumental in laying the foundations for what would become one of the great cities in the United States. Born in 1817, he was an educated man, having studied civil engineering in Dublin before departing for South America. He arrived in Chile and then made his way up the West Coast, learning Spanish along the way and finding work as a land surveyor at various locations before finally reaching San Francisco in 1843.

O'Farrell found employment with the Mexican authorities in 1844 as the official surveyor for Alta California and he was retained by the new United States administration when they took control of the area in 1846. Before his arrival, San Francisco was developing in an uncontrolled fashion, and with ever-increasing numbers of settlers arriving every year the town was badly in need of the kind of considered planning that O'Farrell could provide.

O'Farrell carried out numerous surveys in the area including at San Francisco, Stockton and Sonoma. For San Francisco he produced a detailed street plan for the core of the developing city, including the plotting of Market Street as the main thoroughfare, as well as marking plots for development and naming several of the city's major streets. It was from this plan that San Francisco would develop thereafter, and its completion just before the Gold Rush was especially timely since it provided order to the rapid population growth the city experienced.

O'Farrell settled to the north in Sonoma County where he purchased some 40,000 acres and established Annaly Ranch, named for Anghaile, the ancestral homeland of the O'Farrells in Ireland, now in County Longford. A township developed nearby and was absorbed into the growing agricultural town of Sebastopol. He developed a significant farming enterprise in the area, growing a wide variety of crops as well as breeding cattle and horses and becoming a very wealthy man in the process. He brought his family members from Ireland to live with him including his mother, three brothers and his sister, and donated land for the construction of a Catholic church in nearby Bodega. He died in 1875 having made a major contribution to the development of San Francisco where O'Farrell Street is named in his honour.

THE IRISH DOWN UNDER

The Irish contribution to the cultural heritage of modern Australia and New Zealand is immense, but their early contributions to the bricks and mortar of these new countries was equally important. The Irish were responsible for creating much of the infrastructure that allows cities like Sydney, Auckland and Adelaide to be the thriving metropolises they are today.

MAHONEY & SON

Auckland's architects

Down in New Zealand and its largest city of Auckland you would find it difficult to avoid the work of the influential father and son Irish architects Edward and Thomas Mahoney. Edward Mahoney was born in the garrison town of Ballincollig just west of Cork in 1824, a nephew of the Cork-based architect John Mahoney with whom he trained in the 1840s. As Cork began to feel the full effects of the Great Famine, Edward Mahoney emigrated with his wife and two young children to Australia.

They arrived in Adelaide in 1855 and in 1856 they moved to New Zealand and the city of Auckland. In Auckland, Edward changed the spelling of his surname from Mahony to Mahoney to avoid confusion with a solicitor already established in the city, and set up a building and timber merchants company. His business soon grew and he received his first New Zealand architectural commission in 1861, which allowed him to design the Church of St John the Baptist in the Auckland suburb of Parnell. The simple yet striking gothic revival design was well received and would be the first of many church commissions for Mahoney, most of which still survive today. Among those designed by Edward were the chapel at St Mary's Convent, Ponsonby; St Columba's Presbyterian, Warkworth; St Andrew's, Cambridge; Holy Trinity, Dargaville and St George's in Thames. His son Thomas joined Edward in his practice in 1876. They were prolific designers of buildings across Auckland and further afield in the 1870s and 1880s, including office blocks, apartments, hotels, schools and of course churches.

Edward's best-known work is the Church of the Holy Sepulchre in the Newton suburb, completed in 1880. One of the largest churches in the city, it is known for its warm kauri timber interior and is often regarded as one of the best wooden church interiors in the world. Edward also designed the Auckland Grammar School building and was a founder of the Auckland Institute of Architects.

Edward retired to the large home he built on Harbour Road in St Mary's Bay in 1885 and the business was continued by his son Thomas and another son, Robert. Thomas continued the tradition of church building, though using brick rather than timber. Notable examples include St Benedict's, Newton; all Souls Church, Devonport and St Mary's, Onehunga where another of Edward's sons was parish priest, and the first New Zealand-born Catholic priest to be ordained. Probably Thomas' best-known work today is his extensive renovation and extension of St Patrick's Cathedral in Auckland. Thomas was president of the New Zealand Institute of Architects from 1913 to 1914 and retired shortly afterwards.

ERNEST MCCARTNEY DE BURGH

Hydraulic engineer

In the late 19th and early 20th Centuries Australia was growing rapidly from a collection of small colonial towns to a federal state with a population of millions. Its distance from Europe and tough climate meant it developed much more slowly than North America and faced numerous challenges related to the creation of national infrastructure. Massive distances separated the towns and cities with virtually nothing in between, and providing water to the growing cities was vital if the country was to grow and prosper.

One of the leading Australian engineers of his generation was an Irishman by the name of Ernest McCartney de Burgh. Born in Sandymount, Dublin in 1863, de Burgh went to school in Rathmines before attending the Royal College of Science for Ireland, where he gained the essential scientific knowledge for his future career. After finishing his studies de Burgh worked as a railway engineer in Ireland, but in 1885 he decided to emigrate in search of opportunity and a better life. He arrived in Melbourne aboard the SS Orient, the first in a series of liners to ply the London-Australia route under the famous Orient Line name.

From Melbourne, de Burgh made his way north to Sydney where he found a job working for the New South Wales Department of Public Works and became involved in major civil engineering projects almost immediately. At the time a major bridge building programme was underway to make access between the major inland towns and across to the neighbouring colony of Victoria easier. The many meandering rivers in the area such as the Darling, Murray, Murrumbidgee, Snowy, Hunter and Tweed provided these towns with access to the coast but also prevented easy travel between them. De Burgh was tasked with constructing several bridges that proved a major boost for inland transport in New South Wales including those at Albury, Wagga Wagga, Morpeth and Wentworth.

After several years working on bridges throughout New South Wales, de Burgh was appointed to a senior engineering position in the water department. The Australian colonies had formed a federation in 1901 and Sydney, as the main city in the state of New South Wales, was growing at a rate too rapid to make use of the city's inadequate fresh water supplies, with the city suffering repeated droughts. De Burgh travelled back to Europe to study dam construction in France and Britain before returning to Australia to put what he had learned into practice. He was immediately involved in the Burrinjuck Dam project and many others and by 1913 he was responsible for the growing water supply and sewerage networks of New South Wales. Today he is remembered by the major bridge over the Lane Cove River in Sydney that is named after him.

ALEXANDER BAIN MONCRIEFF

Adelaide's chief engineer

What Ernest de Burgh did for Sydney and New South Wales, his fellow Dubliner and engineer Alexander Bain Moncrieff did for Adelaide and South Australia. Born in 1845, Moncrieff was the eldest son of the well-known Dublin merchant Alexander Rutherford Moncrieff. He attended the Belfast Academy and apprenticed with the Irish Great Southern and Western Railway, where he received an excellent practical engineering education in all aspects of the company. After seven years with the railway he began working at a succession of locomotive works in Drogheda, Glasgow and in England.

However, Moncrieff was ambitious and not satisfied with the opportunities available in Ireland or Britain, so he decided to emigrate to Australia and in 1875 he arrived in Adelaide, the capital of South Australia. In Adelaide he got a job as a draughtsman with the South Australian government. By 1879 he was appointed as an engineer with South Australian Railways working on the extension of the Port Augusta to Oodnadatta line and carried out the design work for coastal improvements around Port Adelaide, which was experiencing a significant increase in shipping at the time. In 1888 he was given the role of Chief Engineer in Adelaide.

In his new role he had responsibility for water, sewage and harbours as well as railways at a critical time for the growing city of Adelaide. Perhaps his most notable achievement was the Barossa Dam completed in 1902. Construction began in 1899 on when finished it was the highest dam in Australia.

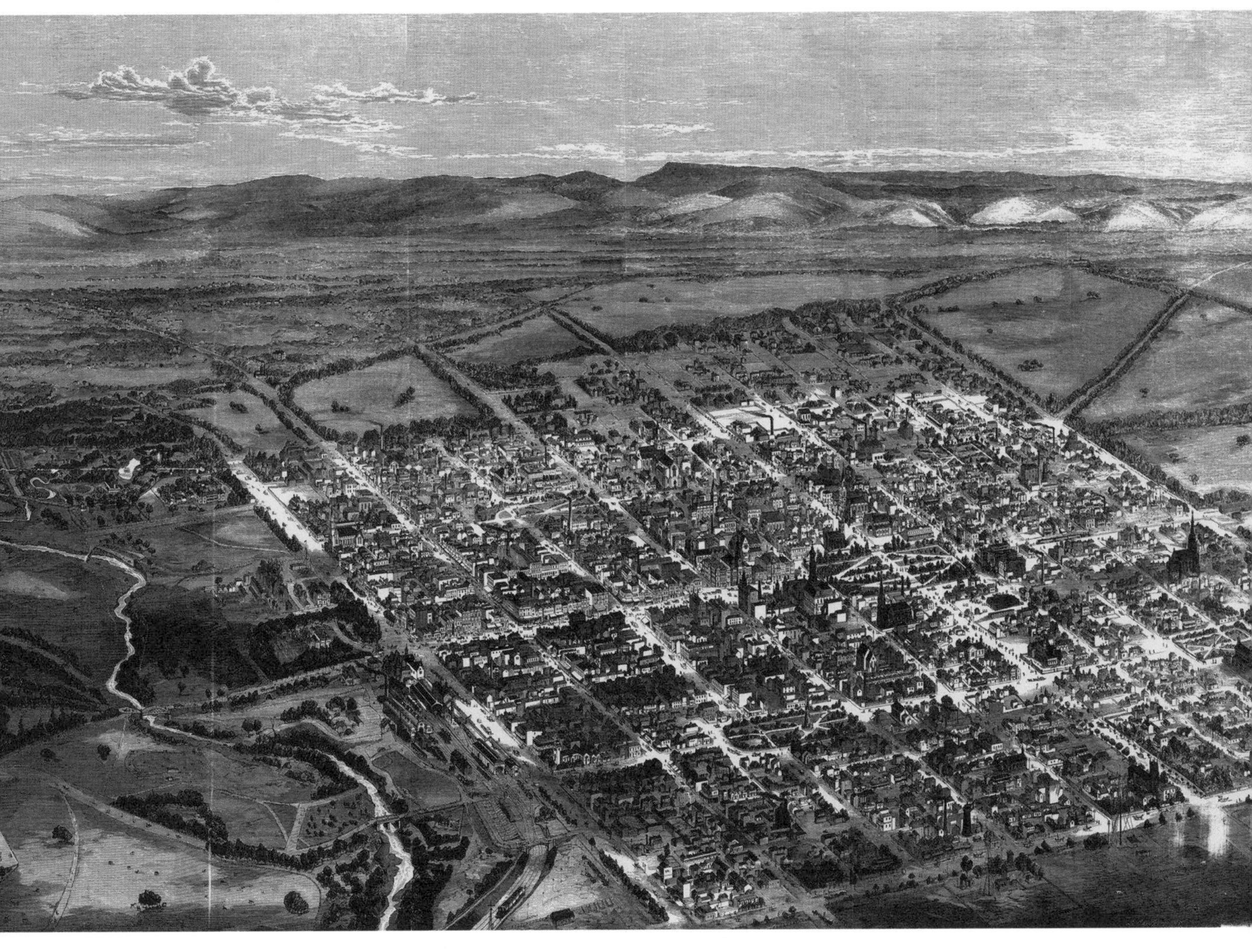

Black and white aerial view of Adelaide in 1876 in Southern Australia. Photo from *Illustrated Sydney News*.

AN IRISH EYE FOR DESIGN

Architecture and design are probably not the first things that come to mind when you think of Ireland but Irish people have made a significant contribution in these fields. Here are a few of these visionaries.

KEVIN ROCHE

Pritzker Prize-winning architect

In an age dominated by 'starchitects', Irish architect Kevin Roche cuts an unassuming figure, content to let his buildings take the limelight. Born in Dublin in 1922, Eamonn Kevin Roche has had an extraordinary career working with some of the most revered architects of the 20th Century before becoming one of the world's most renowned architects himself.

His father, Eamonn Roche moved the family to Mitchelstown in County Cork, where he accepted a job as manager of the Dairygold co-op in the town. Kevin grew up in Mitchelstown and attended senior school at Rockwell College in neighbouring Tipperary. He was not a talented student but did develop an early interest in architecture and as a boy he was "always building things" at the family home. He was accepted at University College Dublin (UCD) to study architecture in a small class of a dozen or so students. After UCD he got a job working with Michael Scott, who would go on to be one of Ireland's leading architects. In 1941 his first commission was to design a piggery at the ever-expanding Dairygold plant by his father. He then went to London where he worked for the modernist Maxwell Fry, and while there came to the decision that he needed a postgraduate qualification to further his career. Setting his sights high he applied to all of the top schools in the USA and was accepted at the Illinois Institute of Technology to study under the modernist pioneer Ludwig Mies Van Der Rohe, one of the leading architects in the world at that time.

Van Der Rohe opened the young Irishman's eyes to the true possibilities of modernism, but Roche was unable to finish the course and dropped out after a year and a half due to a lack of funds. He then took an overnight bus to New York in search of work. At the time the new United Nations headquarters was under construction under the stewardship of Oscar Niemeyer, Le Corbusier, Harrison & Abramovitz. Roche was desperate to gain experience in the project, but he was told there were no vacancies. Instead he was offered a job as a junior draughtsman, which he took in the short-term.

He was considering returning to Europe when he heard that the renowned Finnish architect, Eero Saarinen was seeking apprentices at his practice in Birmingham, Michigan. Roche applied and was shortly after taken on. It would prove to be a fortuitous decision. Saarinen was already a highly regarded architect and had several major commissions, one of which was the massive new General Motors Technical Centre, a project that Roche worked on for several years gaining a vast amount of experience. He later said that under Saarinen's guidance his own philosophy became more humanistic; this people-centred approach coupled with his modernist training under Van Der Rohe would define his own style in later years. It was here that he also met his future partner and friend, John Dinkeloo.

In 1961 Saarinen died suddenly at the age of just 51 with a number of major projects unfinished so Roche, Dinkeloo and their colleagues set about completing them. Among those they finished after his death were the iconic arch in St Louis, the TWA Terminal at JFK Airport, Dulles International Airport near Washington, the John Deere Headquarters in Moline, Illinois and the CBS Headquarters in New York.

Roche and Dinkeloo then moved to the East Coast and set up their own practice, Kevin Roche, John Dinkeloo and Associates in New Haven, Connecticut in 1966. Their first commission was the Oakland Museum of California, one of the first buildings to merge outdoor and indoor spaces and described as one of the first truly green buildings. Roche said that the idea was to create a community space for people to come to, a principle he stuck to with many of his later buildings. He would go on to design many iconic and ground-breaking buildings along with Dinkeloo, including the Ford Foundation building in New York featuring one of the first 'green' public atriums.

Dinkeloo died in 1981 and Roche continued as head of the firm. He has designed more than 50 major projects in all, including the tallest building in Atlanta, major extensions to the New York Metropolitan Museum of Art, the Museum of Jewish Heritage in New York and Dublin's new convention centre. Roche has been recognised with numerous awards for his work, including the Pritzker Architecture Prize, often regarded as the ultimate acclamation in the field. He is without doubt the most successful Irish architect of the modern era.

EILEEN GRAY

The mother of Modernism

One of the most influential figures in the Modern movement in design and architecture was an Irishwoman from County Wexford.

Eileen Gray was born in Enniscorthy in 1878 as Kathleen Eileen Smith. Her father James McLaren Smith was a painter and her mother was Eveleen Pounden, a member of an aristocratic family descended from the Earl of Moray. Encouraged by her father, she developed an interest in art. In 1898 she was among the first women to be admitted to the renowned Slade School of Fine Art, now the art school of University College London (UCL), where she studied painting.

From painting she developed an interest in lacquer work and persuaded a commercial lacquerer in Soho to train her in the art. Lacquer work was particularly popular at the time thanks to the growing Art Deco movement. Following the death of her father in 1902 she moved to Paris, where she continued to study painting, lacquer work and cabinet making. She also took her first steps into commercial work, gaining praise for her lacquered screens and decorative panels.

In 1917 she was commissioned to re-design an apartment in the Rue de Lota for famous milliner Madame Mathieu Lévy. It took Gray four years to complete, during which she created the first of her classic Modern designs, the Bibendum chair, an armchair with a tubular steel frame supporting soft leather tubes that act as the backrest.

In 1922 she opened her own gallery, 'Jean Désert' and began to generate interest from the Paris design community for her screen and carpet designs. During this time she met and began to work with some of the leading proponents of the burgeoning Modernist scene, including Le Corbusier and J.J.P. Oud. Gray's early work in chrome and glass was at the very forefront of Modernism.

Encouraged by Le Corbusier, she then turned her attention to architecture and designed two iconic houses. In 1926 with her friend Jean Badovici she designed and furnished the E-1027 house in Cap-Martin near Monaco, a classic of Modern design. Her work on the project also included her adjustable circular glass and chrome table that would become another icon of Modernist furniture. Then in the early 1930s she designed and furnished herself a new house near Menton, called 'Tempe à Pailla'.

Eileen carried on working into her 80s, converting an old barn in Saint-Tropez into a summerhouse. She died in 1976 at the age of 98 and since her death her work has generated increasing interest. Examples are now on display in London's Victoria & Albert Museum and at The Museum of Modern Art in New York, and there is also a permanent exhibition at the National Museum of Ireland in Dublin. Interest from collectors has also seen her work become highly sought after; in 2009 her 1919 'Dragons Chair' was sold at auction in Paris for a staggering $28.3 million, the second most expensive piece of furniture ever sold from any period and by far the most valuable piece of 20th Century furniture.

FRANCIS FOWKE

Albert Hall architect

An engineer, architect and inventor, Francis Fowke was born into a military family in Ballysillan, Belfast in 1823. He studied at the Royal School in Dungannon, County Tyrone before attending the Royal Military Academy in Woolwich, London. In 1842 he was commissioned into the Royal Engineers where he rose to the rank of captain. Somewhat overlooked in architectural history, Fowke made a major contribution to architecture in Britain and Ireland in the late 19th Century using advanced iron-frame techniques in the construction of some of the largest public buildings of the day.

He served overseas in the Caribbean where he gained extensive engineering experience before returning to Britain where he was employed as a senior architect and engineer in the Royal Engineers. His first big commission was in Plymouth, a major naval base in southwest England where he designed the new Raglan Barracks at Devonport. Following this success Fowke was invited to work on the 1855 Exposition Universelle in Paris.

In 1857 Fowke was appointed as Inspector of the Science and Art Department in London, a role that would lead to his involvement in a series of significant public buildings. He was also sent back to Ireland in 1858 to complete work on the new National Gallery of Ireland in Dublin.

Fowke was a favourite of Prince Albert and through this association he was selected for several major commissions beginning with the new Prince Consort's Library in Aldershot in 1859, a military library for the army base in the town. He also played a significant role in the design of the Victoria & Albert Museum, then known as the South Kensington Museum; he was responsible for its first major expansion, including several galleries, courtyards and a lecture theatre.

In 1862 he was placed in charge of the London International Exhibition and designed the main building for the 21-acre site that is now occupied by the Natural History Museum. Fowke made extensive use of cast iron frames for the massive building that was more than 1,000 feet long and included the two largest domes in the world at that time. More than six million people visited the exhibition but the building was dismantled when the exhibition finished after Parliament voted not to purchase it; instead the materials were sold and used for the construction of the Alexandra Palace.

Fowke's best-known surviving building however is the Royal Albert Hall in London. The hall was part of the complex of public buildings (known as the Albertropolis) in South Kensington proposed by Prince Albert, who wanted to emulate the success of the 1851 Great Exhibition on a more permanent basis. Fowke's design was inspired by the Coliseum in Rome for the exterior but internally made use of the most modern techniques and innovations and construction began in 1867 and was completed in 1871. Before his death he had won the competition to design the new Natural History Museum on the site of his 1862 exhibition building, which was later completed by Alfred Waterhouse.

IRISH ENTERTAINMENT

Ireland and people of Irish descent have made an immeasurable contribution to the world of entertainment. In comedy, music, theatre and film, many of the world's best-known performers past or present have had Irish roots.

SPIKE MILLIGAN

Surreal genius

He was described by the comedian Eddie Izzard as "the godfather of alternative comedy", was a major influence on Monty Python and enjoyed a prolific career on radio and television as well as writing poetry and numerous books. Spike Milligan was arguably the most influential British comedian of the 20th Century. He was born Terence Alan Milligan in India to an Irish father and an English mother and spent his early years in India and Burma while his father served in the British Army. They returned to the UK in 1931 when Spike was 12-years-old and he grew up in Honor Oak in suburban southeast London.

He was called up during the Second World War and served as an artillery gunner seeing action in North Africa and in the Italian campaign where he was wounded at the Battle of Monte Cassino. It was while serving in the army that he started to develop as a comedian, regularly entertaining the troops as a musician and singer and doing improvisational comedy. When he was demobilised he returned to Britain and embarked on a full-time career in entertainment.

Milligan's first major success came as part of the *Goon Show* with Peter Sellers, Harry Secombe and Michael Bentine. The seminal radio show was ground-breaking in its surreal and anarchic approach and soon gathered a dedicated following, propelling Milligan and his colleagues to stardom. Spike became a central performer and main scriptwriter for much of the show's nine-year run, but the pressure of having to write more than 20 half-hour episodes a year finally took its toll on him and he suffered a nervous breakdown. Milligan was to struggle with severe depression for the rest of his life.

From the mid-1950s he began to make forays into television, writing early shows with Peter Sellers and Eric Sykes often with director Richard Lester who went on to work with the Beatles. His television credits include *Don't Spare the Horses, The Idiot Weekly, A Show Called Fred* and *The World of Beachcomber.* In 1969 he wrote and performed in the first of his six Q television series, '*Q5*', that continued until 1982. He also enjoyed success with the children's series *The Ratties* written by his daughter Laura and *Wolves, Witches and Giants* for ITV. Milligan also wrote poetry for both children and adults with his children's poetry in particular being well regarded.

Spike became an Irish citizen in the 1960s and always took pride in his Irish heritage. When he died in 1983 his coffin was draped in the Irish tricolour at his funeral; his head stone bears "Dúirt mé leat go raibh mé breoite" in Irish, meaning 'I told you I was ill'. In 2014 a statue of Milligan was erected in Finchley, north London where he lived for many years.

DAVE ALLEN

The comedian's comedian

The son of an *Irish Times* editor, David Tynan O'Mahony, better known by his stage name, Dave Allen, was born in Dublin in 1936. His education in Ireland's Catholic school system had a major influence on his material in later life, but initially he planned to follow his father into journalism. After working in a junior role at a local newspaper in County Louth he decided to take a different path and at the age of 19 left Ireland for London.

Allen took a summer job as a red coat entertainer at the Butlins holiday camp in Skegness on England's east coast and here he began to learn the ropes as a performer. He also began performing in nightclubs and working men's clubs, creating his first stand-up comedy routines. He appeared on the BBC talent show *New Faces* in 1959 and began to pick up some television presenting work in the early 1960s. After a spell working with the American entertainer Sophie Tucker in South Africa, he decided to try his luck in Australia on her advice.

Allen's Australian tour was a big success and he was offered his own television show, *Tonight with Dave Allen* with Channel 9 as a result. The variety show was popular with Australian audiences but Allen almost blew his big chance when he swore on air at a producer who was trying to get him to wrap up an interview with Peter Cook. He was immediately banned from the airwaves, but the ban did not last long as his popularity further increased. Allen's edgy and topical style was already apparent and he developed a reputation for challenging authority. His signature monologue routine of sitting on a stool, drink in hand and smoking was also part of the show.

After his success in Australia he returned to the UK with a newfound confidence and began to appear regularly on British television and in 1967 was given his own show, *Tonight with Dave Allen* made by ATV. Allen had finally arrived, and the following year he was signed up by the BBC where he made *The Dave Allen Show*, a mixture of sketches and stand-up followed by *Dave Allen at Large* that ran from 1971 to 1979. Allen was now at the cutting edge of British comedy, employing an observational style that was in stark contrast to the gag-based acts of most of his contemporaries. His choice of subject matter also made him stand out as he focussed his satire on the powerful. The Catholic Church was among his most regular targets and as a result he was effectively banned from his native Ireland which was still a deeply conservative country at the time.

He enjoyed further success in the 1990s when he began to be recognised as an early pioneer of what became known as alternative comedy with 1993's *Dave Allen Show* his last series. He died in London in 2005.

GEORGE BERNARD SHAW

Renowned playwright

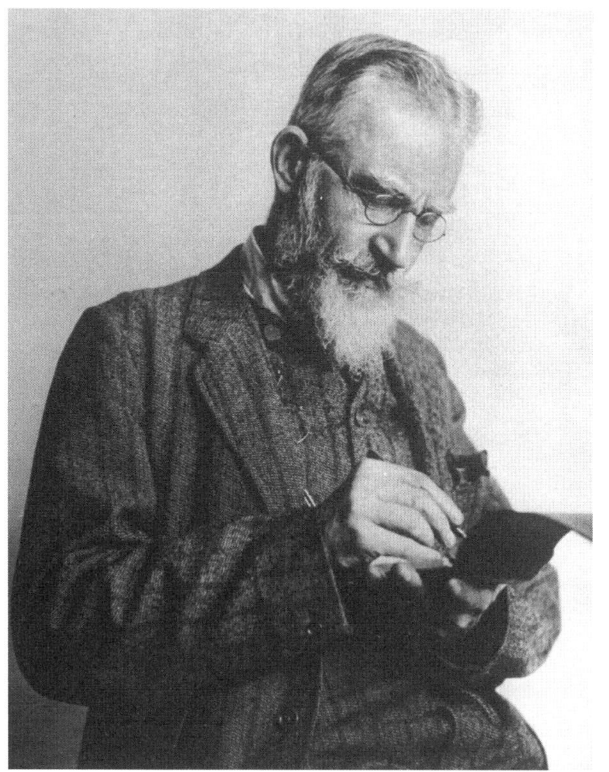

Born in Dublin, George Bernard Shaw was a playwright who is still regarded as one of the greatest dramatists in the English language. Shaw had a deep concern for social injustice and was a member of the Fabian Society; it was this viewpoint that informed much of his best work. Shaw was a critic and essayist as well as a prolific playwright, having written more than 60 plays during his long career, the best known of which today are *Major Barbara, Man and Superman* and *Saint Joan*; he also won an Oscar for the screen adaptation of his own play *Pygmalion*. He was awarded the Nobel Prize for Literature in 1925 and was made a freeman of Dublin in 1946. He continued to write into his 90s and died at home in Hertfordshire, England in 1950 at the age of 94. His legacy is profound and he is cited as one of the originators of both social realism and the theatre of the absurd; plays that owe a debt to Shaw's influence are often described as 'Shavian'.

George Bernard Shaw writing his notebook at the time of the first production of his play "Pygmalion."

SAMUEL BECKETT

Influential playwright

Samuel Beckett. Photo: Roger Pic via Wikimedia Commons

If Bernard Shaw cast a shadow over the first half of 20th Century drama, it was another Irishman, Samuel Beckett, who emerged from it in the second half. Beckett ranks with Shaw as one of the most influential playwrights in history, and having spent much of his life in France he was equally at home writing in French and English. He was born in south Dublin in 1906 and attended the Portora Royal School in Enniskillen, where he excelled as a cricketer and would go on to play while attending Dublin University to study French, Italian, and English. He was a student in Paris for two years, during which time he was introduced to James Joyce and helped him as a researcher; this relationship had a major impact on the young Beckett and instilled in him the confidence to become a writer himself. He began writing poetry, fiction and essays and later returned to Trinity to become a lecturer in 1930.

He left the post in 1931, however and began travelling around Europe, making his first forays into a career as a writer. He moved to Paris permanently in 1938 and was a courier for the French Resistance during the war. It was in the post war years that he wrote many of his best-known works that forged his reputation as an exemplar of Modernism and the absurd. His first play was *Waiting for Godot*, which he completed in French in 1952 and became one of the most influential dramatic works ever written. Other significant plays by Beckett include *Endgame*, 1957; *Krapp's Last Tape*, 1958; *Happy Days*, 1961 and *Footfalls* in 1976. He was awarded the Nobel Prize for Literature in 1969.

NINETTE DE VALOIS

Ballet pioneer

Ballet was something never really seriously contemplated in Britain or Ireland. The French art form perfected by the Russians was thought to be too difficult to really master, that is until a single-minded woman from Wicklow changed everything. Dame Ninette de Valois was born Edris Stannus in 1898 in the picturesque setting of Blessington, County Wicklow. She spent her early years at Baltyboys House on a peninsula overlooking Blessington Lake with views of the Wicklow Mountains. When she was seven she was sent to England to live with her grandmother, and when she turned 10-years-old she began attending ballet lessons.

She took to it instantly and by the time she was 13 had enrolled at a professional dance academy where she adopted the stage name of Ninette de Valois. She was a successful teenage dancer, playing lead roles in several productions before being appointed the principal dancer for the Beecham Opera at the Royal Opera House when she was 21. She studied under a number of teachers in London, including Enrico Cecchetti, and gained extensive experience dancing in pantomimes, operas and various other productions before joining the Ballets Russes under the renowned impresario Sergei Diaghilev in 1923.

By the time she was 26, de Valois was forced to retire from dancing herself as she was suffering from a then undiagnosed case of polio contracted in childhood. Never one to be defeated, however, she soon bounced back from the disappointment by establishing her own ballet school, The Academy of Choreographic Art, in London in 1926. She had learned much from Diaghilev about how to run a ballet school and she put this experience to good use in London. She also established a new school in Dublin, the Abbey Theatre School of Ballet where she produced shows for Terence Gray. She was responsible for running a programme by request from W.B. Yeats, who was a founder of the theatre. Ninette continued in the role from 1927 to 1933, producing several ballets every year.

In London she set about defining a new English ballet with its own independent style and approach. She struck up a friendship with Lilian Baylis who was the owner and manager of the Old Vic Theatre and took over Sadler's Wells Theatre as well. De Valois persuaded Baylis to allow her to stage full-scale productions at the Old Vic, and when the Sadler's Wells reopened following refurbishment, the entire dance school moved into the building and became known as the Sadler's Wells Ballet School; she also established a new ballet company, the Vic-Wells Ballet. The Vic-Wells Ballet Company and school were the forerunners of what would become the Royal Ballet, as well as the Birmingham Royal Ballet and the Royal Ballet School.

Not content with laying the foundations for an entirely new national ballet, de Valois was also active in creating and choreographing many ballets of her own, starting with *Job* in 1931 and including *The Rake's Progress* (1935), *Checkmate* (1937) and many others. Throughout the 1930s, the company was a great success under the direction of de Valois and principal choreographer Frederick Ashton, becoming one of the first companies in the western world to perform the traditional classical ballet repertoire as well as establishing its own unique tradition.

In 1963 she retired as director from the Royal Ballet but remained as head of the school until 1972. She received honorary degrees from Trinity College Dublin as well as the University of London, the University of Sheffield, Durham University, Oxford, Reading, Ulster, Aberdeen and Sussex. She was awarded a CBE, a DBE, received the Order of Merit, the Légion d'Honneur and numerous other state and professional awards from around the world. Today Ninette de Valois is regarded as the most important person in the history of ballet in Britain and Ireland; she was responsible for establishing a new tradition in ballet and founding what is today regarded as one of the world's leading ballet companies.

W.B. YEATS

Ireland's most influential poet

William Butler Yeats looms like a giant over the Irish poetical landscape, noted for his role in the Irish literary revival and in the founding of the Abbey Theatre, he is intrinsically linked with the emergence of the Irish State and Irish nationalism in the early 20th Century. His poetry however reaches far beyond Irish shores and he is without doubt one of the most internationally influential poets of any period. He was born in Dublin in 1865 and is closely associated with County Sligo where he spent many holidays and the county features in much of his work.

Symbolism features heavily in Yeat's work and he is also noted for marrying modernist style with more traditional poetic structures. Among his best known poems are 'Easter 1916', 'Lake Isle of Innisfree', 'Sailing to Byzantium', 'September 1913' and 'The Wild Swans at Coole'. He was awarded the Nobel Prize for Literature in 1923 and died in France in 1939.

SEAMUS HEANEY

Nobel Prize-Winning poet

After W.B. Yeats, Seamus Heaney is probably the next best-known Irish poet to an international audience. He was born in County Derry in 1939, three months after Yeats died, and forged a remarkable career as a poet and academic and was probably the best-known poet in the world during his lifetime. Heaney grew up in the small village of Belaghy and won a scholarship to study at St Columb's College in Derry, then went on to attend Queen's University in Belfast. He became a teacher and lecturer, teaching first at St Joseph's College in Belfast and later at his old college, Queen's.

He began writing poetry early on and was published in the 1960s. He moved to Dublin in 1976 and was poet in residence at Harvard University in Boston from 1988 to 1996. From 1989 to 1994 Heaney was Professor of Poetry at Oxford University and in 1995 he was awarded the Nobel Prize for Literature. Among his best-known poems are 'Death of a Naturalist', 'Mid-term Break', 'Digging' and 'Blackberry Picking'. He was also a translator, notably translating *Beowulf* in 1999.

CECIL DAY-LEWIS

Poet and father of Daniel Day Lewis

Born near Stradbally, County Laois (then known as Queen's County) in 1904, Cecil Day-Lewis was the Poet Laureate of the United Kingdom from 1968 to 1972. His mother died when he was two-years-old and he was subsequently raised by his father in London and spent summers with relatives in County Wexford. He was educated at Sherborne School and then went to Oxford, where he became friends with the poet W. H. Auden and began writing poetry himself.

He became a schoolteacher and worked at various public schools in England before going to work for the Ministry of Information during the Second World War. He continued to write poetry during the war years, and when the war was over he became an editor with the publisher Chatto & Windus. He was also a lecturer in poetry at Cambridge and later a professor at Oxford and at Harvard. He became Poet Laureate in 1968. During a prolific career, Day-Lewis also authored 20 successful crime novels under the pen name Nicholas Blake. Cecil died in 1972 at the age of 68 and was survived by his four children, including the Oscar-winning actor Daniel Day-Lewis.

IRELAND IN THE PICTURE

Often overshadowed by their contemporaries in the worlds of literature and music, the work of Irish painters and photographers is well worth a look, as they have made a very significant contribution to the world of the arts.

MATHEW BRADY

War photojournalist

The Father of American photojournalism, a photographic pioneer and the man responsible for the most valuable photographic record of the American Civil War, Mathew Brady is probably the most important figure in the history of American photography. It was thought he was born in Warren County in Upstate New York to Irish immigrant parents Andrew and Samantha Brady. More recent evidence from census returns, however, suggests that Brady may have been born in Ireland.

He initially trained as a portrait painter under the guidance of William Page and Samuel Morse, and it was through Morse that he was introduced to the new daguerreotype technology, a technique that had recently been developed in France. In 1844 he opened his own photography studio in New York City and began to develop a reputation for photographing famous people; he soon expanded and opened another studio in Washington D.C. where he photographed virtually all of the leading politicians of the era, including Abraham Lincoln.

It is for Brady's work during the American Civil War that he is now best known, providing an incredible record of the conflict from the experiences of the ordinary soldiers, the terrible conditions they endured, the battlefields, commanders and leaders on both sides. When the war broke out in 1861, Brady was already a well-established and respected photographer, having won a number of prestigious national and international awards. His documentary work during the conflict was deliberate and he organised a group of photographers, some of whom were also Irish, to cover as much of the war as possible. Brady and his staff were present at most of the major events of the war and took some of the most iconic images in American history.

In October 1862 Brady exhibited photographs taken by some of his team at the Battle of Antietam that had recently taken place in Maryland. The battle was one of the first major engagements of the Civil War. For the first time the American public saw the reality of war in black and white; the images of the battlefield strewn with dead bodies caused a major sensation at the time.

FRANCIS BACON

Surreal painter

Probably the best-known Irish artist of the later 20th Century, Francis Bacon is widely regarded as a master of the surreal and grotesque depicting human alienation and is one of the most highly regarded painters of the period. He was born at Lower Baggot Street, Dublin in 1909 to English parents and was descended from the brother of the famous 17th Century philosopher of the same name. The young Francis grew up in Ireland and England with periods spent in Kildare, Offaly, Gloucestershire and London.

Bacon knew that he was gay early on and his father's refusal to accept his sexuality led the young Bacon to leave home at the earliest opportunity. He left at the age of 17 and headed for Europe where he visited Berlin, then the continent's Bohemian capital, as well as Paris. He returned to London in the late 1920s and began his artistic career first as an interior designer before moving into furniture and rug design. Art Deco, Cubism and Surrealism were all influential movements at the time and Bacon began to experiment with painting himself, and though completely self-taught, he successfully had his work exhibited by the late 1930s.

After the Second World War, Bacon's work entered a new phase, where he focussed much more on his own emerging surrealist style. It was during this period that he created many of his most renowned works, including Three Studies for Figures at the Base of a Crucifixion and the series of surreal portraits of Pope Innocent. His works mostly focussed on isolation and suffering, reflecting his own experience growing up. He is now regarded as one of the most important painters of the post-World War II period. His Three Studies of Lucian Freud was sold at Christie's in New York in 2013 for $142.4 million.

JIM FITZPATRICK

Che Guevara's portraitist

Of all Irish artists, the one whose work is seen more than any other may not be so well known by name but there is no doubt that an image created by Jim Fitzpatrick in 1968 is among the most recognised by any artist from any era. The image in question is a print of the face of the South American revolutionary Che Guevara, who was also of Irish descent. Fitzpatrick based the print on a photograph taken by Alberto Korda. The black-on-red image of Che's face has since become one of the most recognised images in the world, a symbol of protest and rebellion, and now appears on everything from mugs to posters and t-shirts.

Jim Fitzpatrick himself is a successful artist and illustrator well known for his works based in Celtic and Irish mythology as well as album covers and works focusing on Irish writers and revolutionaries. It is for his iconic 1968 image of Che, however, that he is best known, with art historians ranking it as one of the 10 most recognised images of all time. Fitzpatrick initially didn't seek copyright for it, as he met Che in his youth and was sympathetic to progressive movements around the world who use the image. In the early 2000s however, he decided to seek copyright for the image due to the massive commercial exploitation of it; he also wanted to donate the proceeds to Guevara's family in Cuba. Sometimes known as Viva Che, the image is without doubt the most recognisable work ever produced by an Irish artist.

PAUL KANE

Painter of an unknown America

Born in Mallow, north Cork in 1810, Paul Kane was one of the most important North American artists of the 19th Century. He sailed for Canada with his parents when he was nine-years-old and the family settled in the city of York (now Toronto) on the shores of Lake Ontario. His early working life was spent painting furniture and portraits before he decided to travel to Europe to gain an education in European art. Travelling to London, Paris, Rome, Florence and Venice, Kane returned to Canada four years later, ready to embark on a career as a professional artist.

On his return he met the American painter George Catlin, who greatly influenced the future direction of his work. Catlin was well known for recording the everyday lives of the Native American peoples in great detail and it was something that Kane found deeply inspiring. Kane gained sponsorship from the Hudson's Bay Company and set out in 1845 on extensive travels across the north west of North America across the Great Plains and to the Pacific coast. He worked for three years sketching and documenting what he saw, later producing canvas paintings. He witnessed one of the last great buffalo hunts on the plains and captured the lives of ordinary people that were then under great threat from European immigrants. Kane was very aware that he might have been among the last to witness a pristine landscape that would soon be changed forever..

During the three-year expedition he produced more than 700 sketches as well as written journals and more than 100 oil paintings, most of which were bought by the Canadian government and are on display in the National Gallery, providing an invaluable record of life in the Pacific North West prior to large-scale European settlement. Kane settled down upon his return and he married and had four children. He died suddenly and unexpectedly at home aged 61 after returning from a walk.

EDWARD QUINN

Dublin's photographer

For a life of sophisticated glamour, it would be hard to beat that of Dublin-born photographer Edward Quinn. He was born in 1920, the son of a Guinness worker, and grew up in the Dollymount area of Dublin. Trained as a musician, Quinn joined the Royal Air Force in the Second World War and later secured a job with a charter airline where he met his Swiss wife, Gret. After the war the couple moved to Monaco where Gret worked and Edward returned to the music business.

With little success in music, Quinn decided to try photography instead, and his first published photograph was of an Irish racehorse published in the *Irish Independent*. As the 1950s arrived, the South of France became the destination of choice for movie stars, and Quinn was on hand to photograph them all. Among the many stars he photographed were Grace Kelly, Brigitte Bardot and Aristotle Onassis.

A talented photographer who was well liked by his subjects, Quinn soon developed a strong reputation and his photos began appearing in major newspapers and magazines across the world. During this time Quinn met the artist Pablo Picasso at an exhibition and the two got on well. It was the start of a long friendship during which Quinn took hundreds of photos of Picasso and eventually published four books and made three documentary films on him, all of which were well received.

He remained friends with Picasso right up to his death and through the relationship began working with several other artists, publishing books with Georg Baselitz, Graham Sutherland and Max Ernst as well as photographing Salvador Dali, Francis Bacon and Marc Chagall. A fan of James Joyce, Quinn also produced a book and French film about Joyce's Dublin that were both well received.

A NOVEL IDEA

It's almost a cliché to say that the Irish are great novel writers, and though not every Irish person has the gift of words, there is no doubt that this is the one area where the Irish seem to truly excel. Walk into any 'Irish' bar from Boston to Brisbane, Birmingham to Buenos Aires and you will likely find the walls bedecked with photos and pictures of great Irish writers. There are so many great Irish novelists that it would be impossible to cover them adequately in this book, so here we look at just a few ground-breaking wordsmiths.

JONATHAN SWIFT

The master of satire

More than 300 years after his birth, Jonathan Swift is still widely regarded as an outstanding satirist in the English language. Born in Dublin in 1667, he enjoyed a long career as an essayist and pamphleteer, but most of his works were published anonymously during his lifetime. Swift also wrote *Gulliver's Travels*, the most successful book ever published by an Irish writer; it has never been out of print and has been adapted numerous times.

His parents were both from the west of England but moved to Dublin following the English Civil War. Swift's father died before he was born and his mother returned to England after his birth, leaving him in the care of his uncle Godwin Swift, a lawyer. Thanks to his uncle, Swift was able to attend Kilkenny College and later Trinity College where he received an excellent education.

At around this time there was much political and religious turbulence in Ireland, so Swift headed to England where his mother got him a job as a secretary for the former diplomat and essayist Sir William Temple at Moor Park. It was while at Moor Park that Swift met Esther Johnson, then just eight-years-old, who he maintained a close relationship with all his life and referred to often in his writings as 'Stella'. It has been claimed that Swift secretly married Esther when she was in her 20s, but this has never been proven.

While in England Swift also completed a degree at Oxford, but he was unable to advance his career and decided to become a priest. He returned to Ireland in 1694 and was appointed to the parish of Kilroot, near Carrickfergus on the north shore of Belfast Lough. It was an isolated Anglican community with dwindling numbers in a predominantly Presbyterian area. Swift stayed in the post for less than two years before returning to work for Sir William Temple in England, and continued in the position until Temple's death in 1699. It was during this second period at Moor Park that Swift began to find his feet as a satirist; he spent much of his time working on Temple's memoirs and began writing his own essays as well. He wrote his first significant work, *The Battle of the Books* during this period, a satirical defence of one of Temple's own essays that had come in for public criticism. After Temple's death Swift returned to Ireland to take up a position in the parish of Laracor in County Meath. Looking after another small congregation, Swift had time to write, but it was only after his move to the nearby town of Trim that he began to carve out a career as a satirical writer of note. His earlier composition, *The Battle of the Books* was finally published in 1704 as was *A Tale of a Tub*, a cutting satire of contemporary politics and religion.

Frustrated with the treatment of the Church of Ireland he became a Tory supporter and editor of the pro-tory *Examiner*. Swift left England for good when the Whig party returned to power. Unable to secure a significant position in England he was offered the job of Dean of St Patrick's Cathedral in Dublin in 1713. Bitter at first with his rejection in England, Swift continued to write and over time became a strong supporter of Irish causes, with Ireland and Irish issues becoming an increasingly important part of his work. In 1726 Swift published *Travels into Several Remote Nations of the World, In Four Parts, By*

Lemuel Gulliver, First a Surgeon, and then a Captain of Several Ships better known today by the much briefer title of *Gulliver's Travels*! Written mostly at Woodbrook House, Mountrath in County Laois, the book was an instant hit and has never been out of print since it was first published. A masterful satire on the foibles of human nature it is also seen as a forerunner of the modern novel as well as an early work of fantasy and science fiction. Swift could only enjoy the success of the book for a short time however, as in 1728 Esther Johnson died and his work took on a much darker tone thereafter.

In 1729 Swift published *A Modest Proposal for Preventing the Children of Poor People in Ireland Being a Burden on Their Parents or Country, and for Making Them Beneficial to the Publick*, probably his best-known satirical writing on Ireland. The central conceit is Swift's suggestion that the poor sell their own children as food to escape the grinding poverty experienced by so many at the time. It was a highly shocking piece for the era and created significant reaction in Ireland and in London.

Swift died at the age of 80 in 1745 and was buried in St Patrick's Cathedral in Dublin next to Esther Johnson. With the funds from his estate St Patrick's Hospital for Imbeciles was opened in Dublin 1757; it still operates today as St Patrick's University Hospital. He is remembered by several memorials in Trim where he lived for much of his life and featured on the Irish £10 note for many years; a crater on the moon is also named after him.

SHERIDAN LE FANU

Father of modern horror

Sheridan Le Fanu is often regarded as one of the originators of the modern horror fiction genre. Born in Dublin in 1824 he was a prolific short story and novel writer, and was highly influential in the horror and ghost story genres, as well as being a pioneer of the crime thriller.

He studied law at Trinity College in Dublin and qualified in 1839, but decided soon afterwards to turn to journalism. Le Fanu was already writing ghost stories in his student days, many of which were published in 1880 as *The Purcell Papers*, but his early career was primarily as a journalist and later as a publisher himself. His first published ghost story was 'The Ghost and the Bone-Setter', which appeared in the *Dublin University Magazine* in 1838; he would later own the magazine as well as the *Dublin Evening Mail* for a time. Le Fanu had spent much of his youth in County Limerick where his father was a rector but he settled himself in Dublin in the late 1830s and married Susanna Bennett, with whom he had five children.

His wife's poor health in the 1850s was a source of great stress and anxiety for Le Fanu and is thought by many to have had a major influence on his literary career. In 1858 Susanna died following some sort of severe episode though the contemporary accounts give little indication of the actual cause of death. Le Fanu was deeply affected by the death of his wife, partly blaming himself for being unable to help her, and he stopped writing fiction entirely until 1861, after the death of his mother.

It was that year that he took on the editorship and ownership of the *Dublin University Magazine* and began to publish his own fiction. His work began to attract attention, but his publisher, Richard Bentley, advised him to consider making future works "less Irish" in order to reach a wider audience in England. His most famous book, *Uncle Silas* published in 1864, was set in Derbyshire for this reason. Le Fanu published several novels and numerous short stories from the early 1860s up until his death in 1872. Much of his work would today be characterised as psychological horror, as it relies heavily on implied or imagined terror, rather than overt or obvious supernatural elements. Le Fanu's stories often leave the possibility of more than one explanation for events, leaving it up to the reader to decide what did or did not happen. His much more realistic approach to writing ghost stories and tackling mysterious or supernatural subjects was highly influential both at the time and in subsequent years. Le Fanu's legacy can be seen today in many of the more subtle and intelligent films and books in the genre. He was also not afraid to tackle social, cultural or political issues through his work, and many of Le Fanu's stories can be read on more than one level.

His short story 'Carmilla' is one of the first works in the modern vampire tradition, pre-dating Bram Stoker's *Dracula* by 25 years. The story about a female vampire has been adapted on numerous occasions for film, television, stage and radio and is one of the most influential works in the history of horror. In the later 1860s he again returned to using Ireland as a location for many of his short stories, perhaps due to his ongoing interest in Irish mythology, which also influenced his writing.

MARIA EDGEWORTH

Inventor of the unreliable narrator

Her reputation has faded since her death in 1849, but during her lifetime Maria Edgeworth became the most successful novelist writing in the English language. She was born in Oxfordshire in England, the daughter of Richard Lovell Edgeworth who fathered a total of 22 children with four different wives. Richard was an inventor, educator and intellectual and held progressive ideas for his time about the education of women. Thanks to his support, Maria received a much more comprehensive education that was typical for most girls of the period.

In 1782 she moved to the family estate at Edgeworthstown in County Longford that remained her home for the rest of her life. Maria took on the role of managing the estate and became familiar with the Irish landlord system of the time. Maria was broadly supportive of Catholic emancipation and believed the Irish people should have the right to decide on the proposed union of the country with Britain. The family in general was also regarded as far more understanding to the needs of their tenants than many Anglo-Irish landlords of the period.

Maria's literary career began with the publication of a series of didactical essays on education and the role of women in society in the 1790s, most of which were 'approved' by her father; she later admitted that she really began writing to please him. It was her first novel, *Castle Rackrent*, however, that confirmed her position as a literary talent. The novel was ground-breaking in several ways, introducing the concept of the unreliable narrator. It has also been classified as the first historical novel, the first regional novel and the first saga novel.

The book is also notable for its realism, the use of vernacular language, its sympathetic view of the native Irish and its critical view of the Anglo-Irish landlord class. It was an immediate success and received critical acclaim as well as good sales, with the poet W.B. Yeats describing it as, "one of the most inspired chronicles written in English".

Edgeworth published several more novels over the following years, many of which dealt with the political situation in Ireland, and she became a celebrated lady of letters and by the early 19th Century the best-selling author in the English language. She was a contemporary of Jane Austen, who admired her work, as well as Sir Walter Scott, who she directly inspired. Her 1801 novel *Belinda* was among the first to portray an interracial marriage, though those chapters were changed in later editions.

After receiving criticism from a Jewish American reader for her stereotypical portrayal of Jewish characters, she wrote *Harrington* in 1817, in which she dismantles anti-Semitism and religious prejudice in general. She also wrote for children and was one of the first authors to introduce realism into stories for younger readers. *Helen*, written in 1834, is regarded by many modern scholars as her finest work.

BRAM STOKER

The Dawn of Dracula

Following in the footsteps of Sheridan Le Fanu's trailblazing efforts was another Irish writer who will forever be remembered for writing one particular book, one of the most influential works in the history of fiction; his name was Abraham 'Bram' Stoker and the book was *Dracula*. Stoker was born in Dublin in 1847, one of seven children of Abraham and Charlotte Stoker. He was ill as a child and often bedridden but by the age of seven he was fully recovered. He attended Trinity College in Dublin where he studied mathematics, graduating with honours in 1870. Stoker then joined the civil service like his father before him, but he also took on some additional work in the evenings writing theatrical reviews for Sheridan Le Fanu's *Dublin Evening Mail*.

After spending 10 years working in the civil service, Stoker had clearly decided that he wanted to pursue a more artistic career. Always interested in theatre and literature, he had established a friendship with the famous actor Henry Irving through his work as a reviewer, and Irving encouraged Stoker to write himself. Irving offered Stoker a job as the manager of his production company and London's Lyceum Theatre, which he owned. It was a busy role that required Stoker to travel with the company on tour, but it also inspired him to write. Stoker began writing short stories in the 1870s and published his first novel, *The Snake's Pass* in 1890. He was active in the arts communities in both London and Dublin, and became acquainted with several well-known artists of the day including James Whistler, Arthur Conan Doyle and Oscar Wilde; while touring in America with Irving he also met President Theodore Roosevelt and Walt Whitman.

Dracula was published in 1897 and was followed by *The Lady of the Shroud* in 1909 and *The Lair of the White Worm* in 1911, as well as the well-received *Personal Reminiscences of Henry Irving* that was published following the actor's death in 1906. Stoker's literary output, especially in the later part of his life, was wide ranging and of a high standard. He wrote everything from textbooks to memoirs and short stories, and eventually published 19 novels but it is for his 1897 novel *Dracula* that he will be remembered. It was immediately successful and has continued to grow in popularity ever since its publication.

The novel was inspired by a trip to Whitby that Stoker took while touring with Irving in 1890. The town's dramatic location and ruined abbey were key locations in the novel. He was also inspired by the vampire story *Carmilla* by his compatriot Sheridan Le Fanu and his own life-long interest in folklore from around the world. He died in London in 1912 and since his death *Dracula* has become the most successful horror novel in history and one of the most adapted works of any genre.

ALBERTO BLEST GANA

Father of the Chilean novel

If James Joyce is Irish father of the modern English language novel, then Alberto Blest Gana is a contender for the same title in South America. He was born in 1830 in Santiago, Chile, the son of Irishman William Cunningham Blest, and is widely regarded as a major influence on the modern South American novel. He joined the Chilean army as an engineer then was sent to study in France, and it was while in Europe that he was greatly influenced by the burgeoning realist movement of the time.

He began publishing novels in the 1860s, and his novels were the first in Chile to show the lives of ordinary people in a convincing and realistic way. His novel *Martin Rivas* from 1862 is regarded as the first Chilean novel. His earlier works are far more constrained than those published in his second productive period beginning in the 1890s. After a long career as a diplomat, including serving in London and Paris, he returned home and directed himself once again to literature. It is the works he completed in this period, including *During the Reconquest* (1897), *The Uprooted* (1904) and *Estero the Mad* (1909) that are the foundation of his modern reputation.

JOSEPH FURPHY

Father of the Australian novel

While Blest Gana was busy inventing the Chilean novel, another second-generation Irishman was founding a literary tradition elsewhere in Australia. Joseph Furphy's parents Samuel and Judith had emigrated from County Armagh in 1840 and Joseph was born on a cattle station that his father was working on in Victoria in 1843. His early years were spent living in tough, spartan conditions with no formal education, but by 1850 the family had a more secure footing in their new country and Joseph was able to go to school.

His father set up his own corn merchants business in 1852, which gave the family a permanent base and Joseph and his brother became involved in the family business. He spent his working life in various parts of Victoria working as a farm machinery operator and farm contractor. Reading and writing were an important part of his life from early on, and he began writing poetry in his spare time when he was a young man, winning a local poetry prize in 1867. He also began writing short stories and was published in local newspapers in Victoria.

In 1897 Furphy completed his only novel, *Such Is Life: Being Certain Extracts From The Diary of Tom Collins*, which was published in 1903. The book charts the travails of the tough farming people of Victoria and New South Wales in the late 19th Century and is now widely regarded as the first great Australian novel. He moved to Perth in Western Australia in 1905, where his sons set up an iron foundry.

ARTHUR CONAN DOYLE

Creator of Sherlock Holmes

If Furphy and Blest Gana founded national traditions then our next contender, Arthur Conan Doyle could be said to have founded an entire genre. Scottish by birth, Conan Doyle had strong Irish ancestry. His grandfather on his father's side was the Dublin artist and political cartoonist John Doyle. His mother was Mary Foley who came from a Dublin family and met Arthur's father in Edinburgh.

Doyle attended the prestigious Catholic school Stonyhurst College in England, paid for by one of his uncles. He then returned to Edinburgh to train as a doctor and began writing short stories in his spare time in the 1870s. Doyle served as a doctor on a whaling ship and cargo vessel travelling to east Africa before later setting up his own medical practice in Portsmouth. He did not enjoy great success as a doctor, however, and moved to London with the intention of setting up an opticians, but again the venture did not prosper.

While struggling to secure a reliable income Doyle continued to write, and it was from this hobby that his future was secured. In 1886, his first Sherlock Homes story, *A Study in Scarlett* was accepted for publication in the *Beeton's Christmas Annual*. It was Doyle's big break and would change his life and his fortunes. The story was well received and the character of Sherlock Holmes quickly became a popular hit, with more stories of his exploits with Dr Watson quickly following.

In Holmes, Doyle created one of the all-time greatest detective characters, and was also a major influence on the crime fiction genre that was then in its infancy. Doyle published four Sherlock Holmes novels in his career and more than 50 short stories that were part of a much larger body of work comprising 22 novels, more than 100 short stories, 14 plays and many essays and non-fiction works.

NEWS
VOGUE
THE TIMES

IRELAND IN THE NEWS

The Irish have played a significant role in the development of print journalism around the world. Perhaps it is because of the country's tumultuous birth that the Irish are so often the driving force behind new newspapers when they have emigrated elsewhere; the need to get the word out and find the truth is obviously something that many Irish hold dear.

NELLIE BLY

Investigative journalist

Among the first female journalists to become a household name, Irish American Elizabeth Cochran Seaman, better known by her pen name of Nellie Bly, was at the vanguard of the new investigative reporting that emerged in the later part of the 19th Century. Her father was Michael Cochran, a self-made mill owner from Derry stock who started out as a labourer and became a local judge. She was born in Cochran's Mills, near Pittsburgh.

Elizabeth attended boarding school for a time but was forced to drop out following her father's death in 1870. The large family moved into the city of Pittsburgh in 1880 where Elizabeth helped to run a boarding house with her mother. She was inspired to become a writer when she wrote an angry response to a column in the *Pittsburg Dispatch* that suggested girls were only useful for domestic duties in the home. The paper received several angry replies from women but editor George Madden was particularly taken with one signed by 'Lonely Orphan Girl'. Madden placed an advert in the next edition asking for the writer to come forward and a few days later Elizabeth Cochrane (now spelled with an e) walked in to his office.

Madden asked her to write another article and she came up with 'The Girl Puzzle', a structured defence of the importance and value of women in society. Madden was so impressed that he offered her a job; as was customary for female writers of the time she needed a pen name and so Nellie Bly was born. She began writing investigative pieces for the *Dispatch* that often focused on women, working conditions and other social issues, but found she was often asked to write about 'women's' subjects like fashion and beauty which she was not interested in doing. She then went to Mexico as a foreign correspondent and spent several months in the country, but was forced to return home when she criticised the Mexican authorities for arresting a local journalist; she published the book *Six Months in Mexico* on her return.

Already making a name for herself, Bly left the *Dispatch* in 1887 for New York in search of more challenging work. She was taken on by *The New York World*, owned by Joseph Pulitzer and assigned to an investigative job that would cement her reputation. She gained admittance to the Blackwell Island Women's Lunatic Asylum to report from the inside on allegations of mistreatment of the patients. She managed to convince the authorities she was mentally ill and was admitted. Here she witnessed first-hand the terrible conditions the patients were subjected to, including terrible food, dirty water, filthy conditions and abusive staff.

After spending 10 days in the asylum Bly was released on the request of her editor and set to reporting her findings and later published a book recounting her experiences. *Ten Days in a Mad-House* was a sensation and brought Bly instant fame. Her book spurred a grand jury to investigate asylum conditions, resulting in major changes to the asylum system.

In 1889 she embarked on a round-the-world trip with the aim of beating the fictitious Around the World in Eighty Days achieved by Phileas Fogg in the novel by Jules Verne. Her editor at *The World*, John A. Cockerill, loved the idea and Bly set off from Hoboken, New Jersey in November. At the same time rival publication *Cosmopolitan* sent its own reporter Elizabeth Bisland off around the world in the opposite direction in an attempt to beat Bly. The contest garnered huge interest and readers were offered the prize of a trip to Europe if they could guess when Bly would make it back to New York.

On her way Bly met Jules Verne, the author of the original novel in France and sent short reports back by telegraph to New York. On the final sea leg of her journey across the Pacific she encountered heavy seas that put her behind schedule; Pulitzer hired a private train to carry her across America on the final leg of the journey, arriving in New Jersey on January 25th and completing the almost 22,000 miles in 72 days. Her rival Bisland did not make it back to New York for another four days. Following the record-braking trip Bly had become internationally famous.

Bly took time off from reporting to take over her husband's Iron Clad Manufacturing, where she received several patents. She returned to reporting to cover the First World War and the women's suffrage movement. She died in New York after contracting pneumonia in 1922 aged just 57.

JOHN ROBERT GREGG

Shorthand creator

Of all the Irish people to have a major influence in the world of journalism, one of the most significant was not a journalist at all. Born in County Monaghan in 1867, John Robert Gregg was an educator and inventor of the Gregg Shorthand system, the most popular English language shorthand system, which has been used as an essential tool by journalists the world over since its invention.

As a boy, a teacher injured him when he was caught talking in class and his hearing was affected for the rest of his life. He was unable to participate fully in lessons thereafter because he could not hear what was being said. He was perceived as less intelligent as a result, but taught himself a form of shorthand to make it easier for him to take notes from the snippets of what he could hear.

In adult life Gregg's interest in shorthand continued. He began by translating a French shorthand system and then began developing his own English system. He published the Gregg system in Liverpool in 1888. A moderate success, it did not however become more popular than the already established Pitman system in use in England. Gregg emigrated to the United States in 1893 and it was here that he would find his greatest success. He published the Gregg system in Chicago and it gained popularity almost immediately. He established the Gregg Publishing Company and within a few years Gregg Shorthand had become the most widely used system in the United States.

WILLIAM HOWARD RUSSELL

Knighted Times reporter

Born in Jobstown in Tallaght, Dublin in 1820, William Howard Russell forged a remarkable journalistic career as one of the first, and still regarded by many as one of the best war correspondents in the business. He joined the staff of *The Times* in London as a reporter in 1843 and was assigned to cover the Crimean War. Russell's reports from the front lines were a revelation to the public and for the first time brought the brutal reality of warfare home. His account of the Charge of the Light Brigade was among his most famous pieces. His reports of how British soldiers suffered and were treated at the Siege of Sevastopol, where he coined the phrase 'the thin red line' referring to the line of redcoats facing the enemy, as well as his first-hand account of the Battle of the Alma had a massive impact at home.

By some he was seen as undermining the war effort with Prince Albert saying, "the pen and ink of one miserable scribbler is despoiling the country", while his reports are also credited with directly inspiring Florence Nightingale to become involved with improving the medical provisions for soldiers wounded in action. After Crimea he covered other major events including the 1857 Siege of Lucknow, the Indian Mutiny, the American Civil War, the Austro-Prussian War and the Franco-Prussian War. He was also on board the SS Great Eastern to witness the laying of a new trans-Atlantic telegraph cable and was present at the coronation of Tsar Alexander II of Russia. He retired as a reporter in 1882 and in 1895 he was knighted.

JAMES AUGUSTUS HICKY

'Papa' of the Indian press

A surgeon, gambler, debtor, fearless reporter and pioneer, James Augustus Hicky was a complicated man. He was certainly Irish but from where is unclear, though one account suggests County Cork. What is certain is that in 1780 Hicky was in Calcutta, the capital of British India, and while there he launched India's first ever newspaper. It was called *Hicky's Bengal Gazette* and ran only half-a-dozen block printed pages once a week and caused absolute uproar in the corridors of power. Hicky was reputedly a fearless individual and his Gazette followed in the same manner, so much so that the Governor General of India, Warren Hastings threw him in jail for his troubles.

Undeterred, Hicky kept printing from his jail cell and kept up his popular line of scurrilous gossip regarding the upper classes, including the governor's wife! The troops and traders of the Raj loved it and the paper was exceedingly popular, but it wasn't to last. Hastings had had enough and took away Hicky's materials, further proclaiming that only officially sanctioned newspapers would be allowed in future. Still, Hicky had produced India's very first newspaper; it may have only lasted two years, but it was genuinely independent and he had shown it could be done. Following his example, the indigenous Indian newspaper was born and several others began publishing around the country. Hicky is now often referred to as the 'Papa' of the Indian press.

FREDERICK YORK ST LEGER

Founder of The Cape Times

Almost a hundred years later and thousands of miles to the west, another Irishman launched a newspaper that was again the first of its kind. Frederick York St Leger from Limerick launched the first newspaper in the Cape Colony in South Africa. St Leger was born in 1833 and moved with his wife to South Africa in 1856 where they had eight children. St Leger was headmaster at St Andrew's College in Grahamstown between 1859 and 1862, but by the 1870s he was working as a journalist.

He also became involved in local politics being elected to the Cape Town Assembly in 1875. In 1876 he founded *The Cape Times*, the first daily newspaper in South Africa. The newspaper cost one penny per issue and was an instant hit with the local population, coinciding as it did with the introduction of local democracy in Cape Town. *The Times* soon established itself as Cape Town's paper of record and made a determined effort to hold those in power to account. *The Cape Times* is still published to this day and for a period was owned by the Irish media company, Independent News and Media.

CARMEL SNOW

Fashion editor

Virtually unknown in Ireland, Carmel Snow became the most influential fashion editor of the first half of the 20th Century. As the transformational editor of *Harper's Bazaar*, her impact on the world of fashion was enormous and laid the groundwork for the modern fashion publishing industry. She had a particular gift for spotting raw talent and was responsible for aiding the careers of numerous designers, photographers, writers and models.

She was born Carmel White in Dalkey on the Dublin coast in 1887, one of six children of Peter and Annie White. Her father worked for the Irish Woolen Manufacturing and Export Company and was tasked with organising the Irish pavilion at the World's Columbian Exposition in Chicago in 1893. While in America he became severely ill and died and Carmel's mother was asked if she could complete the job. Amazingly she accepted and set off for America leaving her six children behind in Ireland.

Following the exposition Annie decided to move to America permanently and during the next few years the six children all moved over to join her. Carmel joined her mother in late 1894 when she was seven-years-old but despite her young age never lost her Irish accent during her long career in America. She was sent to a variety of Catholic schools in Iowa, New York and Brussels, and when her education was complete she went to work at her mother's high-end fashion store in Chicago, and later at a new outlet in New York City.

It was during this period that Carmel's real education in the world of fashion took place as she accompanied her mother to fashion and trade shows across America and Europe. She returned to Europe during the First World War and worked for the Red Cross in Paris. Carmel always had a love of writing and when an opportunity arose to go and work for Condé Nast at his *American Vogue* magazine as an assistant editor, she jumped at the chance. In 1926 she was appointed Fashion Editor at the magazine and married George Palen Snow.

However, Carmel began to feel stifled at *Vogue*. She became restless at her lack of advancement and clashed with her conservative editor Edna Chase. She had promised Nast she would turn down any offers from his archrival William Randolph Hearst, but while in hospital giving birth to her third child Brigid in 1932, Carmel accepted an offer from Hearst to become Fashion Editor of his struggling fashion magazine *Harper's Bazaar*. Her decision came as such a shock to Nast that he reportedly got drunk for only the second time in his life and never fully forgave her.

At *Harper's* Carmel finally had the freedom to put her own publishing ideas into practice and began to transform the magazine into the most talked about publication of the day. By 1934 she was Editor-in-Chief and was working with Russian art director Alexey Brodovitch to rewrite the rulebook on how to produce a modern magazine. The new *Harper's* featured bold photography, modern design, photojournalism, and articles by some of the top writers of the day and a thoroughly modern approach.

With photographer Martin Munkacsi she pioneered location fashion shoots, bringing models out of the studio and into the real world – something that had never been done before. At a function in the St Regis Hotel in 1936 she spotted a young woman in a white Chanel dress and flowers in her hair and promptly offered her a job. She was Diana Vreeland, who would go on to become the most celebrated fashion editor of all time at *Vogue*.

She was a vigorous supporter of French fashion when it was at its lowest following the Second World War and was responsible for naming Dior's 1947 collection the 'New Look'. She was also a lifelong supporter of Cristóbal Balenciaga who went on to be revered as the greatest of all European fashion designers. Others whose careers she helped promote in their early days included Richard Avedon, Lauren Bacall, Andy Warhol, Truman Capote and Cecil Beaton.

In 1957 at the age of 70 she was pushed aside at *Harper's*; the world had moved on and it was reluctantly time for her to leave the stage. She was awarded the Légion d'Honneur by France for her efforts in re-establishing French fashion in America following the Second World War.

BEATRICE GRIMSHAW

Travel writer

In an age when it was difficult for women to lead any sort of independent life, Beatrice Grimshaw was a true pioneer and one of the first important female travel writers. She was born in 1870 at Dunmurry, County Antrim, now a suburb of Belfast, and educated at Victoria College as well as in France and London. She came from a well-to-do Church of Ireland family whose home was Dunmurry House, but she showed her independent streak early by converting to Catholicism when she reached adulthood. Grimshaw moved to Dublin where she took on various clerical roles before she began to work as a freelance journalist for a number of magazines, including the *Irish Cyclist*.

Impressed with her work, the publishers made Grimshaw a sub-editor at the *Irish Cyclist* and soon afterwards she was made editor of the much more widely-read *Social Review*. By the early 1900s Grimshaw was already a successful journalist in an era when few women made it into the profession. Despite her comfortable position, she was not content and having always dreamt of travelling to the Pacific Ocean, she decided to leave Dublin to become a travel writer. Grimshaw was appointed as a correspondent with the London-based *Daily Graphic* to file reports from the Pacific islands. On her arrival she reportedly secured her own sailing boat and began her travels, visiting many of the archipelagos in the region.

In 1907 she arrived in Papua New Guinea on assignment with *The Times* and instantly fell in love with the place. Grimshaw stayed there for more than 25 years and even became the first white woman to manage a tobacco plantation. Grimshaw wrote more than 40 books during her career including novels, short stories, essays and travel books. She left New Guinea in 1936 and retired to Kelso in New South Wales, Australia.

JOHN WILLIAMSON

New Zealand newspaper founder

Another Irishman whose journalistic career led to political success was Newry native John Williamson, who became a major figure in the development of New Zealand's largest city of Auckland. Born in 1815 and from a Wesleyan background, Williamson grew up in County Down and worked as an apprentice printer before emigrating to Australia in 1840 with his wife and family. Settling in Sydney, he first worked for the Australian Chronicle and later the Sydney Monitor before moving again to Auckland in New Zealand in 1841.

It was Auckland that would become Williamson's permanent home, and by 1845 he had established his own printing and newspaper business in the city. *The New Zealander* was a popular, progressive newspaper that advocated a pro-Maori stance, in marked contrast to most rival publications. Williamson's progressive and pro-Maori approach led to conflicts with his business partner W.C. Wilson, which eventually led Wilson to leave the business to set up his own newspaper, *The New Zealand Herald. The New Zealander* became a daily newspaper that year and New Zealand's first penny morning newspaper in 1866.

Increasing competition and more demands on his time saw Williamson step away from *The New Zealander* and concentrate instead on his political career. He became Auckland's first full-time politician and sat in the first Auckland Provincial Council as member for Pensioner Settlements (a group of South Auckland suburbs). In 1856 he was elected superintendent of Auckland province and from then on held numerous political posts at local and provincial level. He sat in the second New Zealand parliament in 1855 and represented Auckland West from 1861 to 1870. An independent, he was briefly a Minister Without Portfolio in 1861 and was noted throughout his career for his pro-Maori stance and for his unwavering support for the interests of the Auckland region.

PATRICK LAFCADIO HEARN

Reporter of the Far East

Patrick Lafcadio Hearn was an extraordinary man and writer. He was born on the Greek island of Lefkada (after which he was named) in the Ionians in 1850, then a British protectorate. His father, Irishman Charles Hearn, was the local military surgeon and his mother was from the Greek island of Kythira, south of the Peloponnese. The family moved to Dublin when Patrick was two-years-old and his parents separated soon afterwards, with his mother returning to Greece and his father to a new posting in the Crimea. Patrick never saw his parents again.

Patrick was left in Dublin in the care of his great-aunt Sarah Brenane and received a varied education while also spending summers at her family estate of Tramore in County Waterford. While at boarding school in England, Hearn suffered an injury to his left eye that became infected, causing permanent damage and disfigurement, something he remained conscious of for the rest of his life. By his late teens his great-aunt had run into

The Second Ichikawa Yaozo as a Samurai Standing in the Snow, Katsukawa Shunshō, Edo period. Polychrome woodblock print. The Metropolitan Museum of Art, New York. Public Domain.

financial difficulties and he was sent to London to live with a former maid. When he was 19 he was sent off with a one-way ticket to New York and the address of a family connection in Cincinnati. Upon his arrival, he was offered little help and given just $5 with which to start his new life!

Ever resourceful, Hearn worked a number of jobs before eventually gaining employment as a reporter with the *Cincinnati Enquirer* and later the *Cincinnati Commercial*, two of the largest newspapers in the region. Soon afterwards Hearn moved to New Orleans in Louisiana where he would spend the next 10 years of his life. He began working for magazines like *Harper's* and *Scribner's* as well as for numerous newspapers. He also began writing fiction and translating various works from French and Spanish. Hearn was inspired by the cultural mix in New Orleans and began to take an interest in religion and eastern cultures. He is credited with almost single-handedly fashioning the early 20th Century idea of New Orleans being culturally unique in the United States.

As his reputation grew, Hearn was sent on overseas trips to the West Indies and in 1890 to Japan. This had an immediate impact on Hearn, who fell in love with the country and managed to secure a number of teaching jobs there. At the same time, he began writing extensively about the country and his work began to appear in major newspapers and magazines across the western world. Some of this work is of vital historical importance, providing some of the only detailed reportage of pre-industrial Japan from a western viewpoint.

He married Setsuko Koizumi in Matsue in 1891 and became a Japanese citizen adopting the name Koizumi Yakumo. He became a university lecturer at Tokyo and Waseda universities. His 1904 short story collection of supernatural tales and translations of haiku poetry, *Kwaidan*, had a significant impact in Japan and was later made into a major Japanese film in 1965. During the next few years he also completed a number of important works including *Glimpses of Unfamiliar Japan, Studies of Hand and Soul in the Far East, Japanese Fairy Tales, In Ghostly Japan, Shadowings* and *A Japanese Miscellany*.

A cultural centre at the University of Durham (where he was once a student) in the north of England is dedicated to his memory while there is now also a museum marking his many achievements in his native Lefkada. In Ireland a Japanese gardens has been named after him in Tramore where he spent many childhood summers. In Matsue, the Lafcadio Hearn Museum and his former home are two of the city's most visited sites.

ON FOREIGN FIELDS - THE IRISH AT WAR

With such a fractious history of conflict and rebellion at home, it should not come as much of a surprise to learn that Irish soldiers have played a major role in wars and conflicts around the globe throughout history. From Charlemagne to Napoleon they have served in continental armies as well as playing a key role in the struggle for South and Central America.

THE DUKE OF WELLINGTON

A secret Irishman

Portrait of Arthur Wellesley, 1st Duke of Wellington. Thomas Lawrence, 1814.

Although Wellington is one of Britain's greatest national heroes, the fact that he was Irish by birth underlines the complexity and changing nature of the British and Irish identities over the years. Wellington was born in Dublin, grew up in County Meath and was schooled in Trim. He sat in the Irish parliament, worked in Dublin, commanded thousands of Irish soldiers on the battlefield, and when he was Prime Minister introduced Catholic Emancipation, which made him unpopular within his own party and in England. Bearing all this in mind he seems like the last person to conceal his Irish identity; indeed his family had been in Ireland for hundreds of years and there is even a possibility that he may have been a descendant of Niall of the Nine Hostages.

Part of Ireland's failure to accept him as one of their own probably comes from a famous quote attributed to him in the House of Commons that referred to his Irish heritage: "If a gentleman happens to be born in a stable, it does not follow that he should be called a horse" The problem is that Wellington never said anything of the sort, even though it has been repeated as fact in publications like the *Daily Telegraph*. The quote actually comes from Daniel O'Connell, known as 'The Liberator', who was making a sarcastic comment toward Wellington: "The poor old Duke, what shall I say of him? To be sure he was born in Ireland, but being born in a stable does not make a man a horse." Still, his military achievements, most notably his defeat of Napoleon at Waterloo, firmly secure him among the ranks of Ireland's greatest. Indeed, when he died at the age of 83 in 1852, more than a million people attended his funeral.

BLAIR MAYNE

Proponent of the SAS

Robert Blair 'Paddy' Mayne was one of the most decorated soldiers of the Second World War, an Irish rugby player and founding member of the SAS. Mayne is credited with the very survival of the SAS, due to his exceptional record at a time when the British Army was considering disbanding the unit. He was born in Newtownards, County Down, one of seven children of the wealthy Protestant Mayne family, who owned several businesses in the town.

Mayne was educated at Regent House Grammar School and then at Queen's University, Belfast where he studied law. He was a very successful boxer, becoming the Irish Universities Heavyweight Champion in 1936 and reaching the final of the British Universities Heavyweight Championship where he was beaten on points. He was also a talented golfer and rugby player and also became an officer cadet while at Queens. In 1937 he earned his first of several rugby caps for Ireland and in 1938 he was selected for the British Lions tour of South Africa, playing in all three tests. He graduated in 1939 and joined a law firm in Belfast, but the war interrupted his plans.

Mayne joined the army reserve before the Second World War started and was quickly called up at the outbreak of hostilities. Following the retreat at Dunkirk, the army was looking for recruits to establish a new raiding unit designed to operate behind enemy lines and Mayne volunteered and was selected. He saw action first in North Africa where the newly formed SAS began to make a name for itself destroying enemy aircraft, vehicles, fuel depots and ammunition. Mayne took a leading role and won numerous awards and promotions (though controversially never the Victoria Cross) and is said to have personally destroyed up to 100 aircraft himself.

He saw further action in Sicily, Italy, France, the Netherlands, Belgium, Germany and Norway serving with distinction wherever he went and rising to the rank of Lieutenant Colonel and was commanding officer of the 1st SAS Regiment. He was one of the most decorated soldiers of the war, receiving the Distinguished Service Order with three bars and also being awarded the Legion d'Honneur and the Croix de Guerre by France for his work with the resistance.

Mayne returned to Newtownards after the war and worked as a solicitor and then as secretary to the Incorporated Law Society. He was killed in a car crash in the town in December 1955 at just 40-years-old. Since his death, a statue in his memory has been erected in Conway Square, Newtownards; the town bypass road also bears his name. A campaign has also been launched to see him posthumously awarded the Victoria Cross, which many people feel he was unfairly denied for his wartime service.

MARY ELMES

Righteous Among the Nations

Of all the stories in this book, perhaps the most selfless is that of Mary Elmes, a Cork woman who became the only Irish citizen to be honoured as 'Righteous Among the Nations' by the State of Israel. The Righteous Among the Nations are those non-Jews who risked their lives during the Holocaust to save Jews from extermination by the Nazis; they are remembered at Yad Vashem in Jerusalem, the official memorial to the victims of the Holocaust and one of the city's most visited sites.

Born in 1908, Mary grew up a member of a respected Church of Ireland family in Cork. It was evident from an early age that Mary was a talented student and she went on to study at Trinity College in Dublin, where she was awarded a First Class Honours in Modern Literature in French and Spanish, as well as a Gold Medal given to "candidates of the first class who have shown exceptional merit at degree examinations".

On completing her studies, Mary joined the University of London Ambulance Unit in Spain to help the innocent victims of the vicious ongoing Spanish Civil War. She was posted to Almeria in southern Spain to a children's hospital, but Almeria was bombarded by the German Navy and Mary was moved further north to Alicante where she was put in charge of the hospital.

Things were no easier in Alicante as the fighting raged on and the town sustained one of the worst aerial attacks of the war in May 1938 at the hands of the Italian air force, killing more than 300 civilians. Despite the desperate circumstances, Mary was committed to her work. Her commitment was such that even when her father died back in Cork, she refused to return home as no replacement for her could be found. The Civil War came to an end in April 1939 and a mass exodus of half a million refugees began fleeing to France in order to escape the new nationalist regime. Mary and many of her colleagues went with them, making the tortuous journey across the Pyrenees Mountains between Spain and France. In France they may have escaped the fighting and reprisals but conditions were terrible. Realising that most of the refugees would not return to Spain as they had hoped, the French government finally put in place more organised camps and by the end of May conditions began to improve. Mary set to work caring for the many children who had made the journey and spent much of her time trying to provide some kind of education for them.

In September, the Second World War began when the Wehrmacht invaded Poland. Mary Elmes was based at Camp de Rivesaltes near Perpignan 40km from the Spanish border. As the war progressed and more and more people were detained, this became one of the largest detention centres in France and conditions quickly deteriorated. As an Irish citizen, Mary was able to remain working at the camp when many of her British and American colleagues were forced to leave as their countries entered the war. It was at this time that Jewish prisoners were sent to the Drancy camp near Paris and then on to Auschwitz, where most of them were murdered. Mary and her colleagues soon realised what was happening and they set about saving as many people as they could. Under the Vichy regime, the government was prepared to allow children to be taken from the camp to stay in children's 'colonies' elsewhere, but their parents could not go with them. Mary went around the camp asking parents to let their children go in the hope of saving them from an even worse fate.

When the Nazis took full control in 1942, they also put a stop to children being removed from the camp and those who had already escaped were moved to safer locations high in the Pyrenees where they would not be found by the authorities. Mary also took children from the camp herself and smuggled them across the Spanish border in the boot of her car, with the help of Dr Joseph Weill and Andrée Salomon, two members of the Jewish Children's Aid Society (OSE).

Mary Elmes was arrested in February 1943 and imprisoned in Toulouse and later Fresnes Prison near Paris, but she was released six months later. She continued her humanitarian work until the end of the war despite the huge personal risk to her own safety. It is estimated that she helped save the lives of more than 200 Jewish children during the war.

She was awarded the Legion of Honour, France's highest civil accolade for her efforts during the war but refused to accept it, not wanting any attention for what she did. She often returned to visit Cork throughout her life. On January 23rd, 2013 Yad Vashem recognised Mary Elisabeth Elmes as Righteous Among the Nations.

HUGH O'FLAHERTY

Scarlet Pimpernel of the Vatican

Hugh O'Flaherty was born in Kiskeam, County Cork in 1898 and grew up in the picturesque town of Killarney in County Kerry, where his father James was the steward of the Killarney Golf Club. On completing his schooling, Hugh decided to join the priesthood and studied at Mungret College in Limerick, then went to Rome in 1922 to continue his studies and complete his degree in theology. He was ordained in 1925 and continued his training as a priest.

Hugh then became a successful Vatican diplomat and was assigned to a number of different locations in this capacity including Egypt, Haiti, San Domingo (Dominican Republic) and Czechoslovakia. Back in Rome in 1934, he became a papal chamberlain and subsequently went by the title of monsignor. In Rome he built up extensive contacts in the wider community; he had been a passionate golfer since his boyhood days and counted many local dignitaries among his golfing partners including the former Spanish King Alfonso XIII and Galeazzo Ciano, the foreign minister and Mussolini's son-in-law.

When the Second World War broke out O'Flaherty began to hide Jews, anti-fascists and other opponents of the government at various locations in and around Rome, making use of the extensive contacts he had cultivated. In 1943 his network expanded greatly as Mussolini was removed from power. With the Vatican neutral, O'Flaherty was safe within its confines, but in Rome itself he had to be very careful when making arrangements to hide fugitives. He began going out wearing various disguises and became know as the 'Scarlet Pimpernel of the Vatican'. The SS Obersturmbannführer in Rome, Herbert Kappler, had become aware of O'Flaherty's identity and German officials warned that if he set foot outside of the Vatican he would be shot on sight.

Despite the great danger, O'Flaherty and his associates continued their efforts to hide thousands of people in numerous locations, from monasteries to colleges to private homes all over the city. When Rome was finally liberated in June 1944 there were more than six thousand people successfully hidden in O'Flaherty's clandestine network. O'Flaherty was honoured with the title of Commander of the British Empire and was a recipient of the US Medal of Freedom.

BRENDAN BRACKEN

Churchill's Irishman

Probably the most influential Irishman in Britain in the 20th Century, Brendan Bracken was born in Tipperary in 1901 and grew up in Dublin. His father was Joseph K. Bracken a staunch republican, IRB man and one of the founding members of the GAA. Following the death of his father in 1904 Bracken moved with his mother and three siblings to Dublin, but Bracken was a troublesome child and he was sent to live with a cousin in Australia in 1915 in the hope that he may find some direction in life.

He returned to Ireland in 1919 but began to deny his true heritage often to the point of fabricating an imaginary past for himself. The Irish War of Independence was at its height and the Irish were not popular in Britain to put it mildly; so when he arrived in Liverpool later that year Bracken began presenting himself as an orphaned Australian, claiming his parents had been killed in a bush fire in the outback! In 1920 he managed to enrol at the prestigious Sedbergh School in Yorkshire using his Australian backstory and pretending he was 15-years-old when in fact he was almost 19.

Bracken spent just one term at Sedbergh but it was enough for him to wear 'the old school tie' and present himself as an English public schoolboy. He moved to London in 1922 where he entered the world of publishing. Throughout the 1920s he became more actively involved in politics and was a resolute conservative and developed a life-long friendship with Winston Churchill. Bracken entered politics himself in 1929 when he was unexpectedly elected as the Conservative MP for North Paddington.

When war broke out in 1939 Bracken used all his media skills to lobby for Churchill behind the scenes, and also to convince the man himself, to become Prime Minister. When Churchill took up the role in 1940, he made Bracken his private secretary. Bracken then became crucial in the ongoing talks to secure American financial and material support for the British war effort, before the USA formally entered the conflict at the end of 1941. Due to his media experience, Bracken was appointed as Minister of Information. One of his employees was the writer George Orwell who worked as a civil servant at the BBC and reportedly based his novel *1984* on his experiences, with the omnipotent villain 'Big Brother' being inspired by Bracken's own initials.

When the war ended in 1945 the Labour Party swept to power in a landslide election, but Bracken continued in politics on the backbenches. By 1952 however, he no longer held the same passion for politics and although he was elevated to the House of Lords, he never took his seat there. Instead Bracken concentrated on his publishing interests where he was the editor of the *Economist* and the founder of the current version of the *Financial Times*. He died from cancer at the age of 57 in London in 1958.

BOB COLLIS

Children's advocate

Robert (Bob) Collis, born in Killiney, County Dublin in 1900, was one of the foremost paediatric doctors of his time and was also noted for his work with victims of the Nazi concentration camps. After attending school in Rugby, Collis went on to study at Cambridge and Yale before qualifying as a paediatrician at King's College Hospital in London. He returned to Ireland after the First World War and went to work at Dublin's Rotunda Hospital – the world's first dedicated paediatric hospital.

At the time, services in Irish hospitals were antiquated by international standards and Collis set about establishing a modern neonatal department at the hospital. Collis developed a low-cost design neonatal incubator, which was a major step forward in dealing with premature births. He was also a pioneer in the area of feeding pre-term babies. One of the major problems encountered by doctors was providing the newborn child with sufficient nutrition without causing them undue harm in the process. Collis' solution was to develop a nasal tube feeding technique that was less physically invasive and proved to be major advance in neonatal care.

At the end of the Second World War when the true scale of Nazi inhumanity became apparent, Collis volunteered for the

International Red Cross. He was first sent to Holland from where he put together an aid convoy to travel to the Bergen-Belsen concentration camp. The British Army had just liberated the camp in April 1945, where they found approximately 60,000 prisoners living in deplorable conditions. Many were dying or seriously ill and there were more than 10,000 dead bodies simply left lying around the camp. Collis arrived soon afterwards and was deeply affected by the horrors he witnessed at Belsen. Undeterred, Collis and his colleagues set to work helping evacuate survivors and set up a temporary children's hospital. It was extremely difficult work both emotionally and physically; in the early stages many of the survivors were too malnourished to recover and hundreds continued to die. As time went on, however, those recovering began to outnumber those who were not.

While working in the children's hospital Collis encountered two children, Zoltan and Edit Zinn. The Zinns had been moved to Belsen from the Ravensbrück camp and were the only survivors from their family; their mother had died on the day the camp was liberated and they had lost their father and brother beforehand. When the last survivors from the camp were evacuated, the Zinns were among a small number of children who still did not have a place to go and Collis decided to bring them back to Ireland with him along with four others. He found families for the four other children and adopted the Zinn children himself.

After the war he returned to work in Dublin where he focused on helping children from the city's deprived inner-city neighbourhoods. He helped establish the Marino Cerebral Palsy Clinic in Bray, and here he met Christy Brown, a patient who, with Collis' help, wrote and published *My Left Foot*, an autobiographical novel that would become a literary sensation and was later adapted into an Oscar-winning movie. Collis also authored several books and plays himself.

He later worked in Nigeria and travelled extensively in Africa and India, again focusing on paediatric care for the most vulnerable. Collis died as the result of an accident, falling while out riding near his home in 1975.

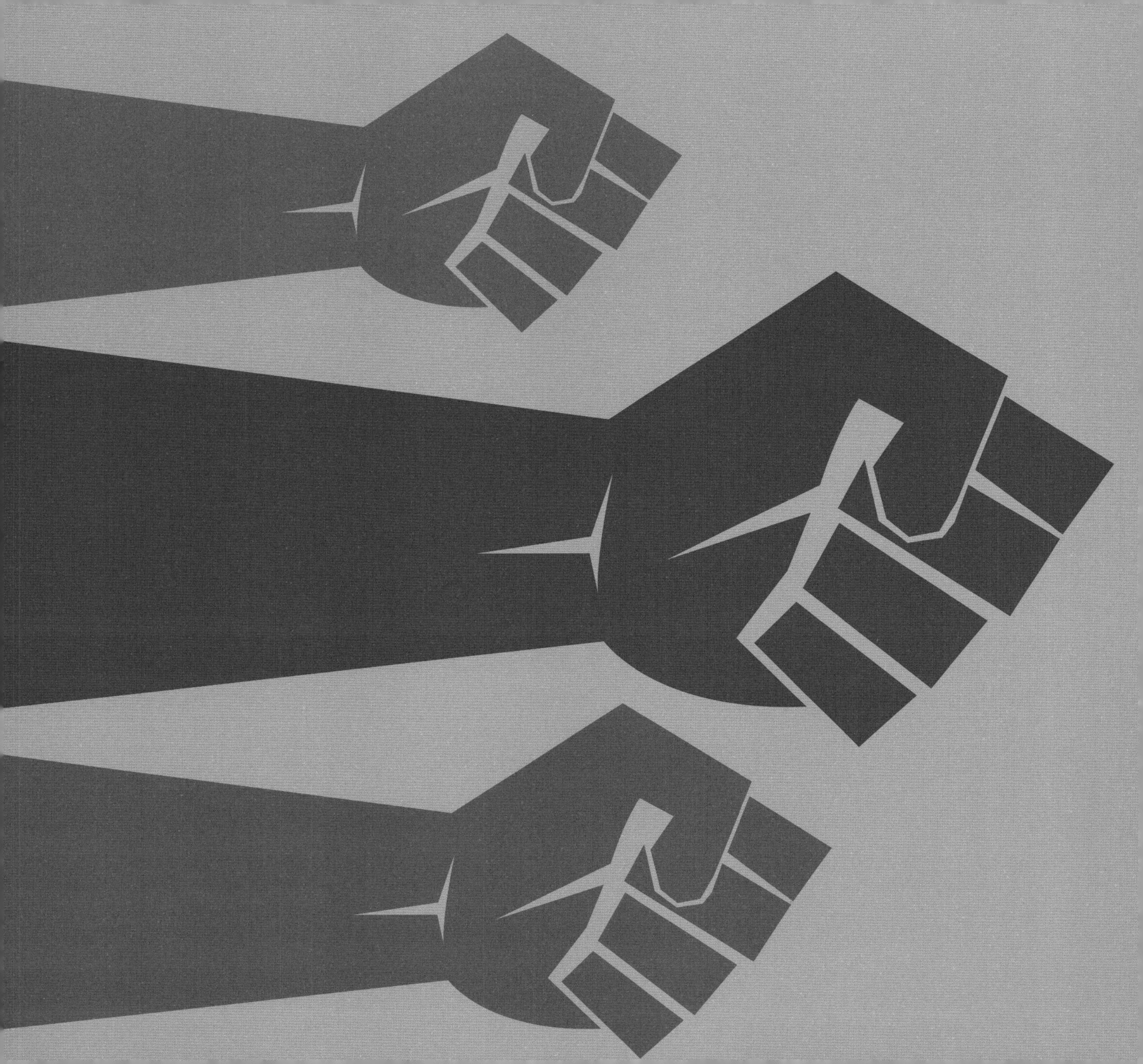

THE IRISH FIGHT FOR THEIR RIGHTS

Irish people and women in particular have played a disproportionate role in fighting for the rights of women and children, workers and the oppressed around the world. Perhaps it was the long shadow of the oppressive society they escaped that drove these people to fight for justice and equality when they arrived in foreign lands. Whatever the reason, they have left a proud legacy and many are remembered today as pioneering activists who led the way for others to follow.

MARY LEE

Suffrage pioneer

A leading campaigner for women's suffrage as well as workers' rights and social justice, Mary Lee was a driving force behind the suffrage campaign that saw women in South Australia gain the vote in 1894. With this decision South Australia became the second major jurisdiction in the world to give women the vote, following New Zealand in 1893.

Lee came from County Monaghan and was the mother of seven children but relatively little is known about her before she emigrated to Australia. Her son Ben moved to Adelaide in 1879 and Mary followed him with her daughter in 1880. By 1883 she was already a well-known figure in the fight for social justice in South Australia, working as a member of the Social Purity Society to successfully lobby to raise the age of consent from 13 to 16 years of age. The society also made progress in fighting child labour and child prostitution and was instrumental in legislation that made it illegal for a man to have sex with a girl under the age of 16.

Next she turned her attention to the working conditions in the state, and a new women's trade union was formed in 1890: The Working Women's Trade Union. Lee served as secretary of this union and helped to initiate relief programmes for the poor as well as campaigning for better conditions in the clothing sector and the mines.

In 1888 the South Australian Women's Suffrage League emerged from the Social Purity League, and a concerted and sustained campaign for women's right to vote began. Lee was co-secretary for six years and was a vocal campaigner, giving speeches and lobbying politicians across South Australia. The League submitted several bills to parliament that all failed, but Lee did not give up. The group presented a petition with more than 11,000 signatures in support of suffrage on the day the Adult Suffrage Bill was voted on in 1894. The move seems to have done the trick and parliament finally voted in favour of women's suffrage.

Following this success, Mary Lee continued to campaign for workers' rights and social justice as well as encouraging female participation in the political system. In 1895 she was nominated to stand for parliament herself but turned down the offer. A memorial to her stands on Adelaide's North Terrace inscribed, "My aim is to leave the world better for women than I find it".

Portrait of Mary Lee. Photo: State Library of South Australia via Wikimedia Commons

MARY FITZGERALD

Mining rights and suffrage advocate

In South Africa, another Irish woman had a significant impact on the trade union movement. Mary Fitzgerald became the first female trade unionist in South Africa. She was born in County Wexford in 1882. She qualified as a shorthand typist while still in Ireland and moved to Cape Town, South Africa with her family in 1900 when her father got a job with the Singer sewing machine company.

There were very few qualified shorthand typists in South Africa and Mary quickly found work, as did the rest of the family. Her younger brother Dennis found employment working on the tramways in Cape Town but was tragically killed in an accident. It was through this tragedy that Mary met his colleague John Fitzgerald and the two went on to marry and raise five children together.

They moved to the booming city of Johannesburg some time later where Mary took a job with the Mine Workers Union as a typist and it was while working there that she became aware of the appalling conditions South African miners were forced to endure. She became involved with the union herself and developed a reputation as an effective public speaker. As well as fighting for the rights of the miners she also joined the South African suffrage movement.

In the early 20th Century there was unrest in South Africa with numerous strikes, lockouts and stoppages occurring as workers agitated for a better treatment, and Mary could often be found arguing the case. During a tram workers' strike in Johannesburg, police charged the workers using pick handles for weapons, some of which were dropped in the fray. Mary picked one up and delivered a defiant speech in favour of workers rights, brandishing the pick handle, which earned her the nickname 'Pick Handle Mary'.

In 1915 she became the first woman to be elected to the Johannesburg City Council and the first woman to hold public office in the city. On her retirement she was presented with a new car and was reputedly the first female car owner and driver in the city. The pick handle she held is now on display at the Museum of Africa in Johannesburg, which faces one of the major public squares in Johannesburg, known as Mary Fitzgerald Square.

LEONORA BARRY

Working rights advocate

Leonora Kearney was born in County Cork in 1849 and was one of the first effective advocates for working women in the United States. Her father moved his family to America in 1852 to escape the ravages of the famine in Ireland. They settled in Pierrepont in New York. Her mother died in 1864 and her father remarried a much younger woman who was only five years Leonora's senior. The change led to tensions and Leonora left home to become a teacher when she was just 15-years-old.

She found work in a local school and soon married fellow immigrant William Barry and the couple moved to Potsdam, New York about 10 miles away. Following her marriage Leonora found she was no longer permitted to teach as a married woman. As a result she was forced to take up manual labour in local factories to supplement the family income and it was this injustice that first drew her attention to worker's rights and, particularly, the rights of women.

The family moved often in search of work and Leonora gave birth to two children who eventually died. She joined the Knights of Labour union in 1884 and within a year had become president of her local district, representing more than 9,000 members. She then represented the district as a delegate to the General Assembly, where she was elected head of the newly created Department of Women's Work.

The aim of the department was to collect information on women's working conditions across the country and lobby for improved pay and conditions. Leonora was one of the first women to hold such an office regionally and the first female national representative in any union. Following her appointment, she embarked on a new life as an investigator, travelling all around the country. She was the first person to compile detailed reports on the working conditions of women across the country and also did valuable work in combatting child labour. In 1893 she delivered a memorable speech at the Columbian exposition in Chicago on 'The Dignity of Labour'.

MOTHER JONES

The champion of the workers

Mary Harris, better known as Mother Jones, was a union activist and campaigner in the USA who was once labelled 'the most dangerous woman in America'. She was born on the north side of Cork in 1837 to an impoverished working-class family. Harris endured unspeakable tragedy and hardship in her own life before becoming one of the most vocal and effective campaigners for better rights and conditions for working people, especially women and children, in American history. Today her achievements are revered in song and theatre, and an annual festival in the city of her birth also keeps her heritage alive.

Her life began in adversity as the Great Famine gripped Ireland, leading to millions of deaths and forcing millions more to emigrate. Her family left like so many others and headed for Toronto, Canada when she was a teenager. Things improved for Harris in North America when she was enrolled in a free school in Toronto and received a basic education. As she reached adulthood, she travelled to the USA and Michigan where she gained employment as a teacher. She then left Michigan before travelling to Chicago and then Memphis, Tennessee where she set up a dressmaking business. It was in Memphis that she met her husband, union activist George E. Jones.

Sadly, Mary's husband and children all died as a result of yellow fever. Realising she could no longer stay in Memphis, she decided to move back to Chicago and opened a dressmaking business. With her life seemingly improving she was struck by yet more tragedy, this time in the form of the Great Chicago Fire of 1871.

The fire destroyed Mary's business and left her with no income, but her dressmaking business had inspired her next move. While working in Chicago, she made dresses for many of the better-off citizens and their families but she also witnessed people in extreme poverty and distress on the streets. It was this inequality, along with the union beliefs of her late husband, that led Jones to take a new course in her life, and she began to work in the union movement, agitating for better pay and conditions and fighting against child labour.

Over the next decades she became a figurehead for workers in the mines, textile mills and on the railways and was affectionately referred to as 'Mother Jones', a name that stuck. She was imprisoned numerous times for defying court orders and travelled the country organising, speaking at rallies and lobbying industrialists and politicians. Jones was a very effective organiser and inspired thousands of workers to take up the fight for better rights. Jones once famously quipped, "pray for the dead and fight like hell for the living".

At a court hearing in West Virginia in 1902, a district attorney called Reese Blizzard described Jones as "the most dangerous woman in America". It was a time of great industrial unrest as workers fought, often literally, for better rights – riots occurred and the authorities shot people on several occasions. Jones testified to Congress about the abuses she witnessed; she led a march of women and children from Pennsylvania to the home of President Theodore Roosevelt on Long Island demanding an end to child labour.

In her later years she settled near Washington D.C. and died at Silver Spring in Maryland in 1930 at the age of 93. One of America's leading liberal magazines, established in 1976 *Mother Jones* was named after her and continues to be influential. In Cork a plaque marks the location where it is believed she was born, and an annual academic festival is held in her honour. She has been the subject of numerous books, articles and documentaries and has been immortalised in theatre and in song by major artists, including Woodie Guthrie and Andy Irvine.

IRISH PHILANTHROPISTS

The Irish have always encountered hardship and poverty both at home and abroad; the years of mass emigration following the famine in particular brought the Irish to many parts of the world where great suffering, disease and destitution were commonplace. Many of those Irish emigrants could not stand by however and these are some of their stories.

ANDREW CARNEY

The Boston philanthropist

The classic self-made man, Andrew Carney didn't have much to start with in life, but that certainly didn't stop him. By the time he died, he had given a substantial portion of his fortune away. He was born in Ballinagh, a small village to the south of Cavan. He gained an apprenticeship as a tailor and in 1816 he left Ireland for America in search of opportunity. Arriving in Boston, Carney found work as a tailor with the firm of Kelley and Hudson on State Street and eventually went into business with Jacob Sleeper, with whom he established the Carney & Sleeper clothing business based in Boston's bustling North End neighbourhood.

Carney & Sleeper became a great success and one of the biggest and best-known clothing firms in the city, winning many lucrative contracts and holding court as one of the first in Boston to sell 'ready made suits'. After spending almost 20 years with the company, Carney decided it was time for a change and left Carney & Sleeper with a large fortune in his pocket. He then became involved in the financial world, helping found two banks and eventually taking a position as director of the John Hancock Life Insurance Company.

Now in his early 50s and always a devout Catholic, Carney seems to have had something of an epiphany because from then on he devoted himself almost entirely to philanthropic and charitable endeavours, which had a profound impact on the growing city of Boston in the process. He was one of the first Catholics in the predominantly (until then) Protestant city to achieve significant wealth as a businessman and he devoted much of his efforts to helping the growing Catholic community and those less fortunate than himself.

He became a benefactor of a home for homeless boys that was run by the Brothers of Charity and made a major donation for a new orphanage run by the Sisters of Charity. He donated to church construction, including paying for the land that was used to build the Cathedral of the Holy Cross in the South End neighbourhood. He was also instrumental in the development of Boston College, now one of America's leading Catholic universities, and became well known around the city for donating to the poor as he went about his daily business.

In 1863 he purchased a large old house in the Dorchester Heights area that had fallen into disrepair. The Howe Mansion, as it was called, became the Carney Hospital for the sick and poor, and he stipulated that it could not discriminate against accepting patients because of their race. The hospital became an important centre for caring for those from Boston who returned injured from the Civil War. Carney died the following year after an extraordinary period of his life where he donated hundreds of thousands of dollars to numerous charities all over Boston. The Carney Hospital still operates today as a community teaching hospital in Dorchester, and Boston College's Carney Hall remembers the merchant and philanthropist who did so much to develop the institution.

THOMAS JOHN BARNARDO

Shepherd of London's children

The son of a Dublin furrier, Thomas John Barnardo underwent a religious conversion at the age of 16 when he became an evangelical Protestant. He decided to travel to China to work as a medical missionary and arrived in London in 1866 to train as a doctor at the London Hospital.

The London that Barnardo encountered was the largest city in the world at the time and was in the throes of rapid expansion due to industrialisation and an explosion in global trade with the British Empire. Thousands were drawn to the city from the countryside in search of work and opportunity. However, London simply could not cope with the numbers, and resources and services were stretched to capacity. Slums grew up, particularly in the East End toward the docks and tens of thousands of people lived in extreme poverty. Disease was rampant due to poor sanitary conditions and a lack of clean drinking water; deadly outbreaks of cholera, typhoid and smallpox were common.

The hospital where Barnardo was training was in the eastern part of the city and he witnessed homeless children wearing little more than rags on a daily basis. Faced with such appalling poverty, Barnardo felt he could not stand by and so established the 'Ragged School' in 1867 designed to give destitute boys a basic education so that they could enter trades and apprenticeships. At first, he kept the school to a limited number of entrants until one day a boy who could not get in when the school was full was later found dead in the street.

The incident profoundly affected Barnardo and from that day on he vowed that "no child should be turned away". He abandoned his plans of going to China and committed to helping the poor children of London. Barnardo worked tirelessly and within a few years he had around a dozen properties in the East End providing food, shelter and accommodation for destitute children.

In 1873 he married fellow evangelist Syrie Louise Elmslie and as a wedding present they were given a lease on a 60-acre site to the east of the city at Barkingside. Here Barnardo established a girl's home where poor girls were trained in domestic service. The site had developed by 1900 into a major centre with 65 cottages, a school, a hospital, a church and even a village green. Barnardo's girls developed a reputation as being among the best trained in domestic service anywhere and were sought after by the wealthiest households.

Thomas and Syrie had seven children together including a disabled daughter and it is thought that this in part inspired him to develop some of the first care facilities in London for children with disabilities.

Thomas died in 1905 at the age of 60 by which time the charity he founded was operating 96 homes caring for vulnerable children and had helped more than 60,000 children in total. Barnardo's today is the largest children's charity in the UK and is still based in Barkingside.

MARGARET HAUGHERY

The Angel of the Delta

Of all the harrowing tales of Irish emigration during the days of the Irish famine, one of the most remarkable is that of a little-known Leitrim woman called Margaret Haughery. Margaret was born in 1813 into an impoverished farming family in County Leitrim, close to the border with Longford and Cavan. She was one of six children and her parents made the heartbreaking decision to leave for America with the three youngest as they could not afford passage for them all, planning to send for the older three when they were settled in the USA.

Margaret was five-years-old when she left with her parents, arriving in Baltimore after an arduous six-month crossing. Almost immediately after arriving, her younger sister died and soon afterwards Baltimore was struck by a lethal yellow fever epidemic that claimed the lives of both of her parents. Her older brother disappeared and Margaret was left orphaned and alone in a strange new world. A Welsh woman named Richards who had befriended her parents during the crossing took her in. When she was old enough, Margaret began working as a domestic servant in Baltimore, having received no formal education.

She met an Irishman called Charles Haughery in Baltimore and in 1835 they were married in Baltimore Cathedral. Charles suffered from ill health and they decided to head south to New Orleans in Louisiana in the hope that the warm climate might be beneficial to him. Charles' health did not improve, however, and on doctor's advice he travelled back to Ireland, for what was planned to be a short stay. Margaret had just given birth to their first child but Charles would never see the baby again, as he died soon after reaching Ireland. Soon afterwards, their child also died from an unspecified disease.

Margaret was only 23-years-old, again in a strange city and had lost her entire family; but she was determined to carry on and secured work at a local orphanage in its laundry facilities. It was while at the Poydras Orphan Asylum that Margaret began her charitable work raising funds for the orphanage; she knew what it was like to be orphaned and saw this as her chance to make a difference.

Thanks to her efforts she was promoted to a fundraising role in the orphanage and took on other responsibilities too, such as minding the institution's own dairy herd and selling on the surplus milk it produced. Margaret showed a flair for business and helped the orphanage clear its debts. With disease a constant problem in sub-tropical New Orleans, she also became well known for helping families in distress and making sure children orphaned by disease were cared for.

As poverty and disease worsened, there was a desperate need for more space for the city's orphans, so Margaret founded a new orphanage that became the St Vincent de Paul Infant Asylum. Her success continued and she opened several more orphanages in the city including the St Elizabeth Orphan Asylum and the Louise Home for Girls. She also helped a local baker with funding for his bakery, taking over the business to keep it from closing. She turned it into a very successful enterprise, providing bread for a network of orphanages across New Orleans, as well as employment for many of the orphans as they became old enough to work.

As the Civil War raged, the numbers of orphans needing help increased dramatically and Haughery became very active in feeding the poor and destitute in the city. When the hostilities finally ceased, she continued with her work and established a new larger bakery that again became very profitable. By this time she was known all over the city for her decades of good work and her contribution to the poor and needy of New Orleans.

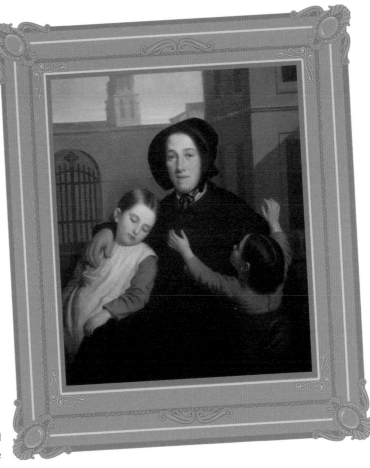

"Margaret" painting by Jacques Amans, New Orleans, c. 1842. Ogden Museum, New Orleans.

Margaret became sick herself in 1881 and suffered a long illness, finally dying in February of 1882 at the age of 69. Her funeral was one of the biggest seen in New Orleans with thousands turning out to mourn the passing of 'the mother of the orphans' with the city mayor leading the procession. In her will she left a large fortune, all to various charities across the city and it was signed with a simple cross as Margaret had never learned to read or write. In 1884 a large statue was erected in New Orleans to her memory in a small park now called Margaret Place. Back in Ireland a recreation of the simple cottage where she was born was erected in the Townland of Tully from where she left in 1818, never to return.

ADVENTUROUS IRISHWOMEN

Bravery can be hard to define, but it can be demonstrated in various ways: by defying convention, risking your own physical safety or taking a stand for what you believe is right. These three remarkable Irish women are clearly some of the bravest women in this book.

KATE SHELLEY

The girl that saved the train

Little known in the country of her birth, a poor farm girl from County Offaly is one of the state of Iowa's greatest heroines; her selfless act of courage in 1881 saving the lives of some two hundred people is a truly impressive feat. The woman in question is Kate Shelley (originally Shelly), born in 1863 near Dunkerrin, Moneygall.

Ireland was suffering the aftermath of the Great Famine, and times were tough for tenant farmer Michael Shelley and his wife Norah, so when Kate was little the family decided to emigrate to the United States where they had relatives in Freeport, Illinois. They moved west from Freeport to the neighbouring state of Iowa settling in Boone County where Michael secured some farmland by Honey Creek, Moingona. They had four more children and seemed to be putting down roots in Iowa when Michael was struck down by Tuberculosis in 1878 and died, and soon afterwards one of the boys drowned in the river. Kate, as the eldest, had to step up and help her mother with the children and the household. Then on the night of July 6th 1881 a violent storm approached Honey Creek that was to change her life.

The sky was dark and sheets of rain driven by a hard wind came through the valley, illuminated by frequent bolts of lightning. The creek was high and Kate kept a constant watch in case the rising waters threatened any of their animals. Then at around 11pm, Kate and her mother could hear the sound of a shunting locomotive coming up from Moingona, probably on its way to check the track. As it approached the Honey Creek Bridge, the loco with four men on board sounded its bell before crashing into the creek – the bridge had been washed away!

Kate knew instantly what had happened but now her concern was for the midnight train that would be heading for that same bridge – she had to get word to the station at Moingona before it was too late. Kate had a problem however: the only way to get there was over the Des Moines River Bridge, one of the highest railway bridges in the country. The bridge also had many wooden slats removed to deter people from trying to cross it on foot.

Still, Kate grabbed a lantern and made for the bridge with less than an hour to get there. It would have been difficult enough in broad daylight on a calm summer's day, but in the atrocious conditions and complete darkness Kate was risking her life by trying to get across. The rain soon swamped the lantern and she found herself fumbling in the dark trying to find the next wooden slat. Because there were so many gaps in the bridge, Kate had to cross the bridge on her hands and knees with just the occasional bolt of lighting to illuminate the way. Despite being buffeted by the wind and rain and cut and bruised from crawling the entire length of the bridge, she finally made to the other side and she trudged on a further two miles to the station to raise the alarm.

LOLA MONTEZ

The Spanish dancer

One of the first women to become internationally famous in her own right was born Eliza Gilbert in Grange, County Sligo in 1821. She is better known by her stage name Lola Montez and by the time of her death she had influenced governments and revolutions, and scandalised society.

Her mother was the illegitimate daughter of a Limerick MP and her father was an officer in the British Army. He accepted a commission to India when Eliza was a child and moved the family. He died from cholera soon after and her mother - who was only 19 - remarried another officer. When Eliza was aged nine she was sent back to England where she gained a reputation as a trouble maker and had to keep moving schools.

While studying in Bath she met her first husband, Lieutenant Thomas James. She was just 16 and the pair eloped when she discovered her mother planned to marry her off to a rich older man. James was also Irish and they initially moved to County Wexford and then to India. However, the marriage failed and soon afterwards she returned to England alone. On the return trip Eliza is claimed to have had an affair with another officer which was cited as evidence in her divorce from James.

Her behaviour scandalised the society of the day and left her with few options for marriage or employment. Ever resourceful, Eliza went to Spain and returned some months later with a new identity, that of Lola Montez – Spanish dancer! Unfortunately, the plan did not quite work as 'Montez' was recognised on her London debut and was booed off the stage. Undeterred she headed for the continent where she quickly gained a reputation as a ravishing Spanish beauty, drawing the admiration of many notable admirers. In Paris she fell in love with Alexandre Dujarier, owner of the *La Presse* newspaper, but he was killed in a duel.

Lola headed to Munich, then capital of the Kingdom of Bavaria, where she gained the immediate attentions of King Ludwig I. They began an affair and Ludwig made Lola a countess. She became a major celebrity and advocated for liberal change in Bavaria antagonising the conservative establishment. When rioters took to the streets, Lola was banished from the kingdom and Ludwig abdicated the throne.

Lola published a book on her experiences in Bavaria leading to even greater notoriety and married again, this time to another British officer named Heald. She was arrested for bigamy however, as her divorce from James stipulated she could not remarry. Lola fled to America where she toured with a very successful play based on the scandals in Bavaria. In California she married again, this time to another Irishman, newspaper owner Patrick Hull but it also didn't last. Hull cited a German doctor in the divorce application and the man was later found shot dead!

Next she headed to Australia with another lover who fell overboard on the return trip. While Down Under she had great success entertaining the crowds who flocked to join the gold rush, but her hard-living ways had now taken their toll and she yearned for a quieter life. She returned to America in 1856 and gave lectures on her experiences, drawing huge crowds wherever she went (including Dublin), and doing outreach work among women who had fallen on hard times. In 1860 she suffered a stroke when she was just 39-years-old and died in New York in January 1861.